PIANO
VOCAL
GUITAR

SELECTIONS FROM

What makes a song great? Is it the melody, the lyrics?

Can a song's greatness be measured by its cultural impact or its influence on other musicians? Or can we just say a song is great because it makes us want to dance? Or, just because...

Choosing the 100 greatest songs was an overwhelming proposition so VH1 sent ballots to over 700 musicians, songwriters, disc jockeys and radio programmers and asked them to vote on the 100 greatest songs of rock and roll. The votes were calculated and the songs were ranked, producing the following list. While it's possible to debate the placement of some of these songs (too high or too low is an argument for you to enjoy), it's difficult to deny that each is an achievement on some level and deserving of the accolade "a great song," as these are truly great songs.

ISBN 0-634-03789-7

7777 W. Bluemound Rd. P.O. Box 13819 Milwaukee, WI 53213

Visit Hal Leonard Online at
www.halleonard.com

RANK	SONG	ARTIST	YEAR
1.	(I Can't Get No) Satisfaction*	*The Rolling Stones*	1965
2.	Respect	*Aretha Franklin*	1967
3.	Stairway to Heaven*	*Led Zeppelin*	1971
4.	Like a Rolling Stone	*Bob Dylan*	1965
5.	Born to Run	*Bruce Springsteen*	1975
6.	Hotel California	*Eagles*	1977
7.	Light My Fire	*The Doors*	1967
8.	Good Vibrations	*The Beach Boys*	1966
9.	Hey Jude	*The Beatles*	1968
10.	Imagine	*John Lennon with The Plastic Ono Band*	1971
11.	Louie, Louie	*The Kingsmen*	1963
12.	Yesterday	*The Beatles*	1965
13.	My Generation	*The Who*	1966
14.	What's Going On	*Marvin Gaye*	1971
15.	Johnny B. Goode	*Chuck Berry*	1958
16.	Layla	*Derek and The Dominos*	1971
17.	Won't Get Fooled Again*	*The Who*	1971
18.	Jailhouse Rock	*Elvis Presley*	1957
19.	American Pie	*Don McLean*	1972
20.	A Day in the Life	*The Beatles*	1967
21.	I Got You (I Feel Good)	*James Brown*	1965
22.	Superstition	*Stevie Wonder*	1972
23.	I Want to Hold Your Hand	*The Beatles*	1964
24.	Brown Sugar*	*The Rolling Stones*	1971
25.	Purple Haze	*The Jimi Hendrix Experience*	1967
26.	Sympathy for the Devil*	*The Rolling Stones*	1968
27.	Bohemian Rhapsody	*Queen*	1976
28.	You Really Got Me	*The Kinks*	1964
29.	Oh, Pretty Woman	*Roy Orbison*	1964
30.	Bridge Over Troubled Water	*Simon & Garfunkel*	1970
31.	Hound Dog	*Elvis Presley*	1956
32.	Let It Be	*The Beatles*	1970
33.	(Sittin' On) The Dock of the Bay	*Otis Redding*	1968
34.	All Along the Watchtower	*The Jimi Hendrix Experience*	1968
35.	Walk This Way	*Aerosmith*	1977
36.	My Girl	*The Temptations*	1965
37.	Rock Around the Clock	*Bill Haley and His Comets*	1955
38.	I Heard It Through the Grapevine	*Marvin Gaye*	1968
39.	Proud Mary	*Creedence Clearwater Revival*	1969
40.	Born to Be Wild	*Steppenwolf*	1968
41.	Smells Like Teen Spirit	*Nirvana*	1992
42.	Every Breath You Take	*The Police*	1983
43.	What'd I Say	*Ray Charles*	1959
44.	Free Bird	*Lynyrd Skynyrd*	1975
45.	That'll Be the Day	*The Crickets*	1957
46.	Whole Lotta Love*	*Led Zeppelin*	1969
47.	Dream On	*Aerosmith*	1973
48.	California Dreamin'	*The Mamas & The Papas*	1966
49.	Brown Eyed Girl	*Van Morrison*	1967
50.	Wild Thing	*The Troggs*	1966

RANK	SONG	ARTIST	YEAR
51.	Suite: Judy Blue Eyes	*Crosby, Stills & Nash*	1969
52.	Beat It	*Michael Jackson*	1983
53.	Great Balls of Fire	*Jerry Lee Lewis*	1958
54.	Stayin' Alive	*Bee Gees*	1978
55.	For What It's Worth	*The Buffalo Springfield*	1967
56.	Blowin' in the Wind	*Bob Dylan*	1963
57.	Twist and Shout	*The Beatles*	1964
58.	Piano Man	*Billy Joel*	1974
59.	She Loves You	*The Beatles*	1964
60.	Space Oddity	*David Bowie*	1973
61.	Strawberry Fields Forever	*The Beatles*	1967
62.	Kashmir*	*Led Zeppelin*	1975
63.	Crazy	*Patsy Cline*	1961
64.	London Calling	*The Clash*	1979
65.	Jumpin' Jack Flash*	*The Rolling Stones*	1968
66.	Rock and Roll*	*Led Zeppelin*	1972
67.	Let's Stay Together	*Al Green*	1972
68.	All Shook Up	*Elvis Presley*	1957
69.	Maggie May	*Rod Stewart*	1971
70.	Your Song	*Elton John*	1971
71.	Heartbreak Hotel	*Elvis Presley*	1956
72.	God Only Knows	*The Beach Boys*	1966
73.	The Twist	*Chubby Checker*	1960
74.	Good Golly Miss Molly	*Little Richard*	1958
75.	Sunshine of Your Love	*Cream*	1968
76.	California Girls	*The Beach Boys*	1965
77.	Summertime Blues	*Eddie Cochran*	1958
78.	Blue Suede Shoes	*Carl Perkins*	1956
79.	A Hard Day's Night	*The Beatles*	1964
80.	Fire and Rain	*James Taylor*	1970
81.	Gloria	*Them*	1966
82.	Sexual Healing	*Marvin Gaye*	1983
83.	Start Me Up	*The Rolling Stones*	1981
84.	More Than a Feeling	*Boston*	1976
85.	Roxanne	*The Police*	1979
86.	We Are the Champions	*Queen*	1977
87.	Tangled Up in Blue	*Bob Dylan*	1975
88.	Somebody to Love	*Jefferson Airplane*	1967
89.	Stand by Me	*Ben E. King*	1961
90.	Whole Lotta Shakin' Goin' On*	*Jerry Lee Lewis*	1957
91.	You Shook Me All Night Long	*AC/DC*	1980
92.	When Doves Cry	*Prince*	1984
93.	In the Midnight Hour	*Wilson Pickett*	1965
94.	Gimme Some Lovin'	*Spencer Davis Group*	1967
95.	Jump	*Van Halen*	1984
96.	Thunder Road	*Bruce Springsteen*	1975
97.	No Woman No Cry	*Bob Marley*	1974
98.	La Bamba	*Ritchie Valens*	1959
99.	We've Only Just Begun	*The Carpenters*	1970
100.	Papa Was a Rollin' Stone	*The Temptations*	1972

*Omitted from this publication because of licensing restrictions.

CONTENTS

ALL ALONG THE WATCHTOWER

Words and Music by
BOB DYLAN

A B C#m B A B
There's too much con - fu - sion.
C#m B A B C#m B
I can't get no re - lief.
Busi - ness men they ah ah they
A B C#m B A B
drink my wine.
Plow men dig my earth.
C#m B A B C#m B
None will lev - el own the vine.
No - bod - y upp - ing its worth.

A
B
C#m
Hey hey. No rea - son to get ex - cit - ed,
the thief he kind - ly spoke.
There are man - y here a - mong us
who feel that life is but a joke.
But uh,
but you and I we've been through that, but uh,

C#m
B
A
B
C#m
B
and this is not our fate.
So let us not talk false-
ly now.
The ho-ur's get-tin' late.
Hey, well
all a-long the watch-tow-er
prin-cess kept the view,
while all the wom-en came and went

C#m
B
A
B
C#m
B
their foot ser-vants, too.
Well ah oh out-side in the cold
A
B
C#m
B
A
B
dis-tance uh
a wild-cat did growl.
C#m
B
A
B
C#m
B
Two rid-ers were ap-proach-in'
and the wind be-gan to howl.
A
B
C#m
B
A
B
Hey.
Ah.

C♯m
B
A
B
All a - long the watch - tow -
er.
Have you ev - er must be a way out
here?
Repeat ad lib.
and Fade

ALL SHOOK UP

Words and Music by OTIS BLACKWELL
and ELVIS PRESLEY

E♭7
F7
B♭
E♭7
mm oh, oh, yeah, yeah!
B♭
My hands are shak - y and my knees are weak, I
can't seem to stand on my own two feet.
Who do you thank when you
have such luck? I'm in love!
I'm all shook up! Mm

E♭7
F7
B♭
E♭7
mm oh, oh, yeah, yeah!
B♭
E♭7
Please don't ask what's on my mind, I'm a
tongue gets tied when I try to speak, my
B♭
lit - tle mixed up but I'm feel - in' fine. When I'm
in - sides shake like a leaf on a tree. There's
E♭7
near that girl that I love best, My
on - ly one cure for this soul of mine, that's to

F7
Bb
heart beats so it scares me to death!
have the girl that I love so fine!
She touched my hand, what a
chill I got, her kiss-es are like a vol-ca-no that's hot! I'm
proud to say she's my but-ter-cup. I'm in love! I'm
Eb7
F7
all shook up! Mm mm oh, oh, yeah,

1
B♭ E♭7 B♭
yeah! My
2
B♭
yeah! I'm
E♭7 F7
all shook up! Mm mm oh, oh, yeah,
B♭ E♭7
yeah! I'm all shook up! Mm mm oh,
F7 B♭
oh, yeah, yeah! I'm all shook up!

BEAT IT

Words and Music by
MICHAEL JACKSON

Moderately fast
N.C.
mf
Em
D
Em
They told him, "Don't you ev - er come a - round here. Don't wan - na see your face; you bet - ter
They're out to get you. Bet - ter leave while you can. Don't wan - na be a boy; you wan - na
Instrumental
D
C
D
dis - ap - pear." The fi - re's in their eyes and their words are real - ly clear. So
be a man. You wan - na stay a - live; bet - ter do what you can. So

Original key: E♭ minor. This edition has been transposed up one half-step to be more playable.

Em
D
Em
beat it, just beat it. You bet - ter run; you bet - ter
beat it, just beat it. You have to show them that you're
D
Em
D
do what you can. Don't wan - na see no blood. Don't be a ma - cho man. You
real - ly not scared. You're play - in' with your life. This ain't no "truth or dare." They'll
C
D
Em
wan - na be tough; bet - ter do what you can. So beat it. But you
kick you, then they'll beat you, then they'll tell you it's fair. So beat it. But you
D
To Coda
Em
D
wan - na be bad.
wan - na be bad. Just beat it, beat it. No
End instrumental

Em
D
Em
one wants to be de - feat - ed.
Show - in' how funk - y, strong
D
Em
1 D
is your fight.
It does - n't mat - ter who's wrong or right. Just
Em
D
Em
D
beat it, just beat it, just beat it, just beat it.
2 D
Em
D
Em
wrong or right. Just beat it, beat it.
No one wants to be de - feat -

D
Em
D
- ed. Show - in' how funk - y, strong is your fight. It
Em
D
N.C.
does - n't mat - ter who's wrong or right. Just beat it. Beat it.
Beat it. Beat it.
1
2
D.S. al Coda

CODA
Em
D
Em
beat it,
beat it.
No one wants to be de - feat -
D
Em
D
- ed.
Show - in' how funk - y, strong is your fight.
It
Em
D
Repeat and Fade
Optional Ending
Em
does - n't mat - ter who's wrong or right.
Just
beat it.

AMERICAN PIE

Words and Music by
DON McLEAN

Em
Am
Em
Am
But Feb-ru-ar-y made me shiv-er with ev-'ry pa-per I'd de-liv-er.
C
G/B
Am
C
D
Bad news on the door-step I could-n't take one more step I
G
D/F#
Em
Am7
D
can't re-mem-ber if I cried when I read a-bout his wid-owed bride,
G
D/F#
Em
C
D7
G
C
Some-thing touched me deep in-side the day the mu-sic died.

Moderately
G
G
C
G
D
So bye - bye, Miss A - mer - i - can Pie Drove my
G
C
G
D
Chev - y to the lev - ee but the lev - ee was dry. Them
G
C
G
D
To Coda
good ole boys were drink - in' whis - key and rye Sing - in'
Em
A7
this - 'll be the day that I die,

Em
D7
This - 'll be the day that I die.
G
Am
1. Did you write the book of love and do you
2.-4. See additional lyrics
C
Am
Em
have faith in God a - bove?
If the Bi - ble tells
D
G
D/F♯
you so
Now do you be - lieve in

Em
Am7
C
rock and roll. Can mu - sic save your mor - tal soul and
Em
A7
D
can you teach me how to dance real slow?
Em
D
Well, I know that you're in love with him 'cause I
Em
D
C
G
saw you danc - in' in the gym, You both kicked off your shoes.

A7
C
D7
Man, I dig those rhy - thm and blues. I was a
G
D/F#
Em
Am
lone - ly teen - age bronc - in' buck with a pink car - na - tion and a
C
G
D/F#
Em
pick - up truck. But I knew I was out of luck the day
C
D7
G
C
the mu - sic died.

1,2,3
G
D7
4
G
D7
G
C
I start - ed sing - ing
He was sing - in' bye - bye, Miss A -
G
D
G
C
G
D
mer - i - can Pie
Drove my Chev - y to the lev - ee but the lev - ee was dry.
Them
G
C
G
D
good ole boys
were drink - in' whis - key and rye
Sing - in'
Em
A7
Em
this -'ll be the day that I
die,
This -'ll be the day that I

D7
die.
rit.
Freely
G
D/F#
Em
Am
C
I met a girl who sang the blues and I asked her for some hap - py news, But
Em
D
she just smiled and turned a - way.
G
D/F#
Em
G
Am
G/B
C
I went down to the sa - cred store where I heard the mu - sic years be - fore But the

Em
C
D
man there said the mu - sic would - n't play.
And
Em
Am
Em
Am
in the streets the chil - dren screamed, the lov - ers cried and the po - ets dreamed. But
C
G/B
Am
C
D
G
D/F♯
Em
G/B
not a word was spo - ken the church bells all were bro-ken. And the three men I ad - mire most, the
C
D7
G
D/F♯
Em
Fa - ther, Son and the Ho - ly Ghost, They caught the last train for the coast the

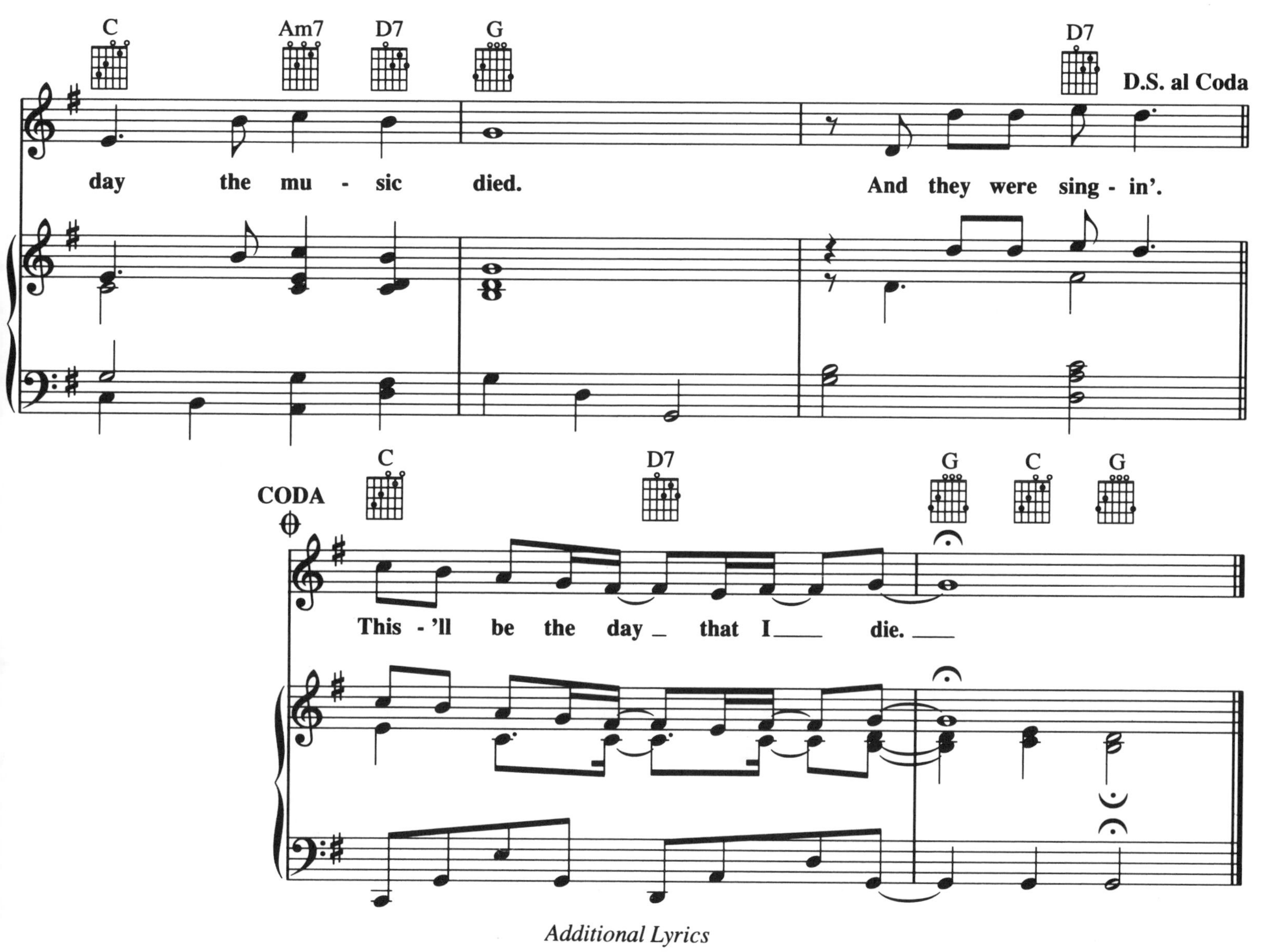
C
Am7
D7
G
D7
D.S. al Coda
day the mu - sic died.
And they were sing - in'.
CODA
C
D7
G
C
G
This - 'll be the day that I die.

Additional Lyrics

2. Now for ten years we've been on our own,
And moss grows fat on a rollin' stone
But that's not how it used to be
When the jester sang for the king and queen
In a coat he borrowed from James Dean
And a voice that came from you and me
Oh and while the king was looking down,
The jester stole his thorny crown
The courtroom was adjourned,
No verdict was returned
And while Lenin read a book on Marx
The quartet practiced in the park
And we sang dirges in the dark
The day the music died
We were singin'... bye-bye... etc.

3. Helter-skelter in the summer swelter
The birds flew off with a fallout shelter
Eight miles high and fallin' fast,
it landed foul on the grass
The players tried for a forward pass,
With the jester on the sidelines in a cast
Now the half-time air was sweet perfume
While the sergeants played a marching tune
We all got up to dance
But we never got the chance
'Cause the players tried to take the field,
The marching band refused to yield
Do you recall what was revealed
The day the music died
We started singin'... bye-bye... etc.

4. And there we were all in one place,
A generation lost in space
With no time left to start again
So come on, Jack be nimble, Jack be quick,
Jack Flash sat on a candlestick
'Cause fire is the devil's only friend
And as I watched him on the stage
My hands were clenched in fists of rage
No angel born in hell
Could break that Satan's spell
And as the flames climbed high into the night
To light the sacrificial rite
I saw Satan laughing with delight
The day the music died
He was singin'... bye-bye... etc.

BLOWIN' IN THE WIND

Words and Music by
BOB DYLAN

D G G/F♯
How man - y seas must a white
Yes, and how man - y years can some peo -
Yes, and how man - y ears must
A/E D
dove sail be - fore she
- ple ex - ist be - fore they're al - lowed
one man have be - fore he can hear
G D/F♯ A/E
sleeps in the sand? Yes, and how
to be free? Yes, and how
peo - ple cry? Yes, and how
D G G/F♯ A/E
man - y times must the can - non - balls fly
man - y times can a man turn his head
man - y deaths will it take 'til he knows

D
G
D/F♯
be - fore they are for - ev - er banned?
and pre - tend that he just does - n't see?
that too man - y peo - ple have died?
D
G
G/F♯
The an - swer, my friend,
A/E
A/C♯
D
G
is blow - in' in the wind.
The an -
G/F♯
A/E
D
- swer is blow - in' in the wind.

G
D/F♯
A
D
G
1, 2
G/F♯
A/C♯
D
Yes, and
3
Slower
G/F♯
A/E
rit.
D

BLUE SUEDE SHOES

Words and Music by
CARL LEE PERKINS

Brightly, not too fast
F
B♭
F
mf
N.C.
C
N.C.
F7
N.C.
F7
Well, it's one for the mon - ey, two for the show,
N.C.
B♭7
three to get read - y, now go, cat, go! But don't you

F
step on my blue suede shoes.
You can
C
B♭
F
B♭7
do an - y - thing but lay off of my blue suede shoes.
F
C
N.C.
F7
N.C.
F7
Well, you can knock me down, step on my face,
burn my house, steal my car,
N.C.
F7
N.C.
slan - der my name all o - ver the place;
drink my ci - der from my old fruit jar;
Do an - y - thing that you

F7
N.C.
B♭7
want to do, but uh - uh, hon - ey, lay off of my shoes. Don't you
F
step on my blue suede shoes. You can
C
B♭
1
F
B♭7
do an - y - thing but lay off of my blue suede shoes.
F
C
N.C.
2
F
B♭7
F
F7♯9
Well, you can shoes.

BORN TO BE WILD

Words and Music by
MARS BONFIRE
Moderate Rock
Eb
mf
Get your mo - tor run - ning.
I like smoke and light - ning,
Head out on the high - way
heav - y met - al thun - der
look - ing for ad - ven - ture
rac - ing in the wind
in what -
and the
ev - er comes our way.
feel - ing that I'm un - der.
Gb
Ab
Yeah, dar - ling, gon - na

Eb
Gb
Ab
Eb
make it hap - pen, take the world in a love em - brace.
Gb
Ab
Eb
Gb
Ab
Fire all of your guns at once and ex - plode in - to space.
1
Eb
Bb
2
Eb
Like a true na-ture child we were born,
Gb
Ab
born to be wild. We have climbed so high,

G♭
E♭
D♭
never want to die.
Born to be wild.
E♭
D♭
E♭
D♭
Born to be wild.
E♭
D♭
1
2
E♭
D♭
E♭
D♭
Repeat and Fade
Born to be wild.

BOHEMIAN RHAPSODY

Words and Music by
FREDDIE MERCURY

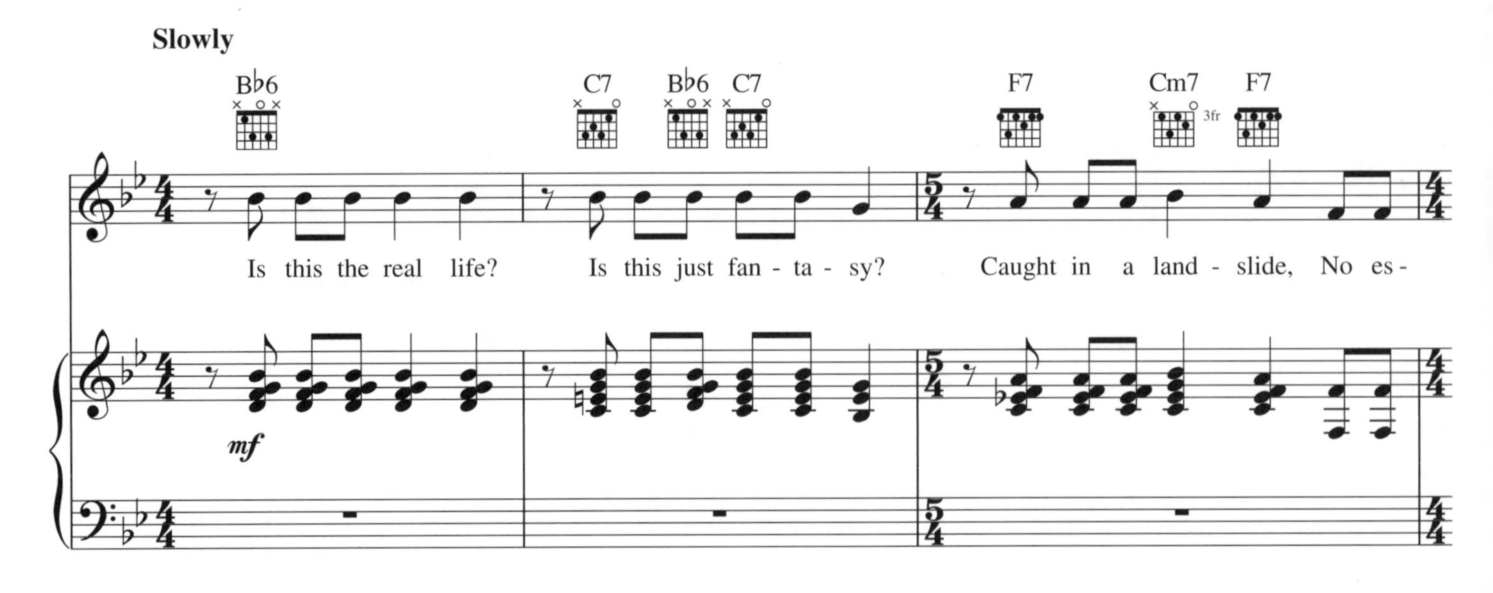

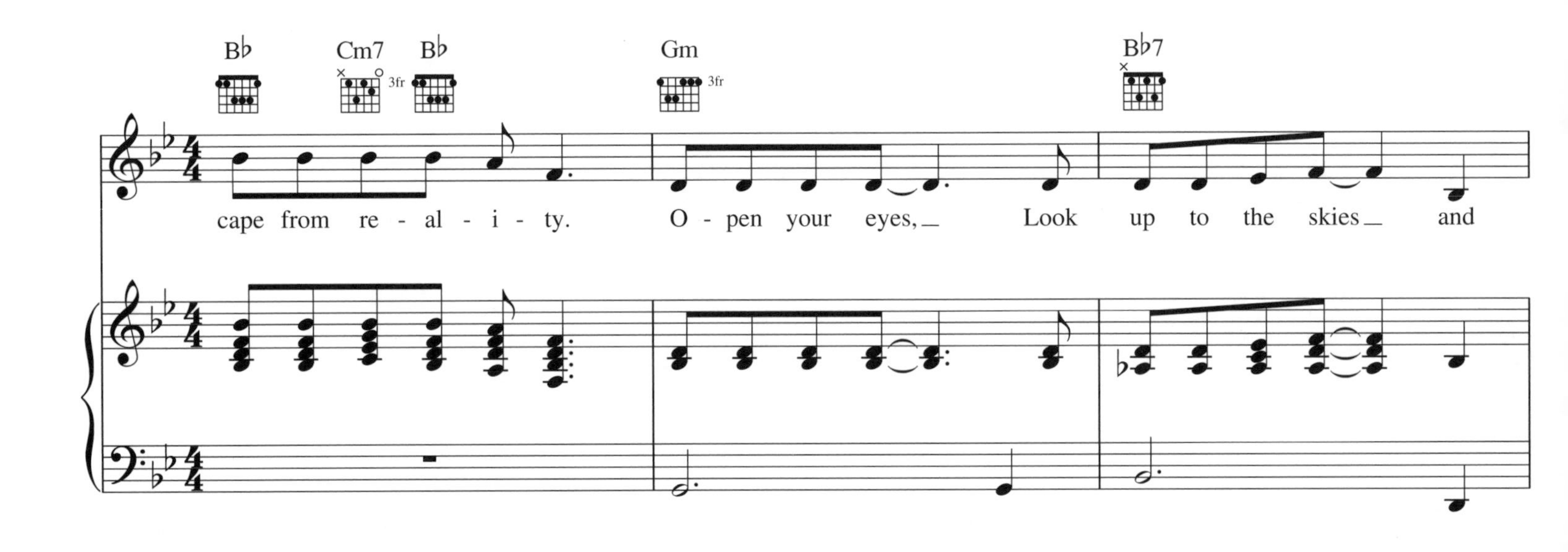

B
B♭
A
B♭
B
B♭
A
B♭
E♭
3fr
B♭/D
eas - y come, eas - y go, Lit - tle high, lit - tle low, An - y way the wind blows
C♯dim7
F/C
F
B♭
does - n't real - ly mat - ter to me, to me.
B♭
Gm
3fr
Cm
3fr
Ma - ma just killed a man Put a gun a - gainst his head, pulled my
Too late, my time has come, Sends shiv - ers down my spine, bod - y's
F
B♭
Gm
3fr
trig - ger, now he's dead. Ma - ma, life had just be - gun, But
ach - ing all the time. Good - bye, ev'- ry - bod - y I've got to go, Got - ta

Cm
B+
E♭/B
F/A
Fm/A♭
E♭
B♭/D
now I've gone and thrown it all a - way.
leave you all be - hind and face the truth.
Ma - ma
Ma - ma,
ooh,
ooh,
Cm
Fm
B♭
Did - n't mean to make you cry. If I'm not back a - gain this time to -
I don't want to die, I some - times wish I'd nev - er been born at
1
E♭
B♭/D
Cm
A♭m
E♭
A♭/E♭
E♭
mor - row, car - ry on, car - ry on as if noth - ing real - ly mat - ters.
E♭dim
Fm7/E♭
B♭

2
E♭
B♭/D
Cm
Fm
3fr
all.
6
B♭7
E♭
Gm/D
Cm
Fm
D♭
D♭/C♭
B♭m
L'istesso tempo (♪ = ♩)
A
D/A
Adim
I see a lit - tle sil - hou - et - to of a man, Scar - a -

D/A A D/A A Adim A D/A A D♭/A♭ A♭
4fr
Chorus:
mouche, Scar - a - mouche, will you do the Fan - dan - go. Thun - der - bolt and light - ning,
f
C/G E A
N.C.
ver - y, ver - y fright - 'ning me. (Gal - li - le - o.) Gal - li - le - o. (Gal - li - le - o.) Gal - li -
le - o, Gal - li - le - o fig - a - ro Mag - ni - fi - co.
(let ring - - - - - - - - - - - - -)
B B♭ A B♭ B B♭ A B♭ A♭/E♭ E♭ E♭dim E♭
3fr
Solo: I'm just a poor boy and no - bod - y loves me.
Chorus:
He's just a poor boy
mf
f

Ab/Eb
Eb
Ebdim
Eb
Ab
Eb/G
F
Bb
from a poor fam - i - ly. Spare him his life from this mon - stros - i - ty.
mf
Ab
Eb/G
F#dim7
Fm7
B
Bb
A
Bb
B
Bb
A
Bb
Solo: Eas - y come, eas - y go, will you let me go, Bis -
f
Eb
Bb
Eb
Bb
Chorus:
mil - lah! No, we will not let you go. (Let him go!) Bis - mil - lah! We
Eb
Bb
will not let you go. (Let him go!) Bis - mil - lah! We will not let you go. (Let me go.)

G♭7
(Let me go)
(Let me go.)
Will not let you go.
Will not let you go.
Ah.
Bm A D D♭ G♭ B♭ E♭
N.C.
3fr
Solo:
Chorus:
No, no, no, no, no, no, no. (Oh ma - ma mi - a ma - ma mi - a.) Ma - ma
E♭
B♭ E♭ A♭ D Gm
4fr
mi - a, let me go. Be - el - ze - bub has a dev - il put a - side for
B♭
me, for me, for me.

E♭
3fr
F7
B♭7
E♭/B♭
6fr
So you think you can
B♭
E♭
3fr
B♭
D♭
stone me and spit in my eye.
B♭7
E♭/B♭
6fr
B♭
E♭
3fr
A♭
4fr
So you think you can love me and leave me to die.

Fm
Bb
Fm
Oh, baby, can't do this to me,
Bb
Fm7
Bb
Fm7
Bb
baby, Just got-ta get out, Just got-ta get right out-ta
Eb
Bb7
here.
poco a poco rit. e dim.
Slowly, a tempo
Eb
Bb/D
Cm
G/B
Cm
G7/B
Cm
Bb7
Eb
D
Gm
mf

A♭
E♭
Cm
Gm
Cm
Gm
4fr
3fr
Noth - ing real - ly mat - ters,
An - y - one can see,
Cm
A♭m
B♭11
E♭
A♭/E♭
Noth - ing real - ly mat - ters,
Noth - ing real - ly mat - ters to me.
rit.
a tempo
E♭
E♭dim7
B♭/D
B♭m/D♭
C7
C7♭9
C7
F
B♭
F/A
A♭dim7
Gm7
F
6fr
An - y way the wind blows.
poco a poco rit. e dim.
p

BORN TO RUN

Words and Music by
BRUCE SPRINGSTEEN

With a driving beat ♩ = 144
E
A
1.
Bsus
B
mf
2.
Bsus
B
E
In the day we sweat it out on the streets of a
A
Bsus
E
run - a - way A - mer - i - can dream.
At night we ride through man -
A
B
- sions of glo - ry in su - i - cide ma - chines.

A
E/G♯
F♯m
E/G♯
Sprung from cag - es on High-way 9, chrome wheeled, fuel in-ject-ed, and step-pin' out o-ver the line.
E
D/E
A
E/G♯
Oh, ba-by, this town rips the bones from your back. It's a
F♯m
E/G♯
E
C♯m
death trap, it's a su-i-cide rap. We got-ta get out while we're young. 'Cause tramps
A
B
E
like us, ba-by, we were born to run.
f
(Instrumental solo ad lib. . . .

A
Bsus
B
E
A
Bsus
B
Wen-dy,
mf
. . . end solo)
E
A
let me in, I wan-na be your friend, I wan-na guard your dreams and
Bsus
E
vi-sions. Just wrap your legs 'round these vel - vet rims, and

A
Bsus
A
strap your hands 'cross my en - gines. To - geth - er we could
E/G♯
F♯m
E/G♯
E
break this trap. We'll run till we drop, and, ba - by, we'll nev - er go back.
D/E
A
E/G♯
F♯m
Oh, will you walk with me out on the wire? 'Cause, ba - by I'm just a scared and
E/G♯
E
C♯m
A
lone - ly rid - er, but I got - ta know how it feels, I want to know if love is wild, babe, I

B
E
want to know if love is real.
A
Bsus
B
E
(Spoken:) Oh, come and show me.
A
Bsus
B
E
A
f Instrumental solo (with drive)

B
E
A
B
C♯m
B
E
Bm7
Be-
mf
Dsus
D
Dsus
D
Gsus
G
yond the Pal - ace hem - i - pow-ered drones_
scream down the bou - le - vard._
Gsus
G
Asus
A
Asus
A
Girls comb their hair_ in rear - view
(Spoken:)
mir-rors and the

Csus
C
Csus
C
Dsus
D
boys try to look so hard. (Sung:) The a - muse-ment park ris - es
Dsus
D
Gsus
G
Gsus
G
bold and stark as kids are hud-dled on the beach in a mist. I wan-na
Asus
A
Asus
A
Csus
C
Csus
C
die with you, Wen-dy, on the streets to - night in an ev - er - last - ing kiss.
Fsus
F
Fsus
F
Fsus
F
C
f
(Instrumental solo ad lib. . . .

C
Fsus
F
Fsus
F
F♯sus
F♯
F♯sus
F♯
N.C.
The
. . . end solo)
E
A
high - ways jammed with bro - ken he - roes on a last chance pow - er drive.

Bsus
B
E
Ev - 'ry - bod - y's out on the run to - night, but there's
A
Bsus
B
A
no place left to hide. To - geth - er, Wen - dy, we can
E/G♯
F♯m
E/G♯
E
live with the sad - ness, I'll love you with all the mad - ness in my soul.
D/E
A
E/G♯
F♯m
Oh, some day, girl, I don't know when, we're gon - na get to that place where we

E/G♯
E
C♯m
A
real - ly wan - na go, and we'll walk in the sun. But till then, tramps like us,
B
E
C♯m
ba - by, we were born_ to run!_ Ah, hon - ey
A
B
E
tramps like us, ba - by, we were born_ to run!_
C♯m
A
B
E
_ Come on,_ Wen-dy. Tramps like us, ba-by, we were born to run!_

A
Bsus
B
E
(Optional) Woh.
Hm,
oh, oh, oh, oh.
Woh, oh, oh, oh, oh,
Hm.
Woh.
Woh.
Woh, oh, oh, oh, oh.
ritard.

BRIDGE OVER TROUBLED WATER

Words and Music by
PAUL SIMON

E♭ A♭ 4fr E♭ B♭/D Cm 3fr B♭
I'm on your side. Oh,
I'll take your part. Oh,
B♭9 E♭ Gm/D E♭/D♭ E♭7 E♭9/G 5fr A♭ 4fr F
3
when times get rough, and friends just can't be found,
when dark - ness comes, and pain is all a - round,
B♭ E♭ B♭ A♭ 4fr B♭/A♭ Adim7 E♭/B♭ C7sus C7
like a bridge o - ver trou - bled wa - ter,
A♭ 4fr G7/B Cm 3fr E♭ B♭ A♭ 4fr B♭/A♭ Adim7
1
E♭/B♭ C7sus C7
I will lay me down. Like a bridge o - ver trou - bled wa - ter,

A♭
G7/B
E♭
E♭7
A♭/E♭
I will lay me down.
E♭
E♭7
A♭/E♭
E♭
A♭/E♭
When you're
2
E♭/B♭
Cm
A♭
G+
G
Cm
F7
trou - bled wa - ter, I will lay me down.
E♭/B♭
B♭
A♭
Cm
A♭
A♭m
E♭

A♭/E♭ E♭ E♭7 A♭/E♭ E♭ A♭/E♭
Sail on
E♭ A♭/E♭ E♭ A♭ 4fr D♭ 4fr A♭/C
sil - ver girl, sail on by. Your time has
E♭ Fm7 E♭ A♭ 4fr E♭ A♭ 4fr
come to shine. All your dreams are on their way.
E♭ B♭/D Cm 3fr B♭ E♭ Gm/D
See how they shine. Oh, if you need a friend

E♭7/D♭ E♭7 E♭7/F E♭9/G A♭ F B♭ E♭ B♭ A♭ B♭/A♭ Adim7
I'm sail - ing right be - hind. Like a bridge o - ver
E♭/B♭ Cm A♭ G7/B Cm E♭7 A♭ A♭maj7 F7/A
trou - bled wa - ter, I will ease your mind. Like a bridge o - ver
E♭/B♭ Cm A♭ G7 Cm F9
trou - bled wa - ter, I will ease your mind.
E♭/B♭ B♭ A♭ Cm A♭ A♭m E♭
rall.

BROWN EYED GIRL

Words and Music by
VAN MORRISON

Eb
Bb7
Eb
Ab
skip-ping and a jump-ing. In the mis - ty morn - ing fog _ with
Eb
Bb7
Ab
Bb7
our hearts a-thump - in', and you, my brown eyed
Eb
Cm
Ab
Bb7
girl. You, my brown eyed girl.
Eb
Bb7
Do you re-mem - ber when we used to sing:

Additional Lyrics

2. Whatever happened to Tuesday and so slow
Going down the old mine with a transistor radio
Standing in the sunlight laughing
Hiding behind a rainbow's wall
Slipping and a-sliding
All along the water fall
With you, my brown eyed girl
You, my brown eyed girl.
Do you remember when we used to sing:
Chorus

3. So hard to find my way, now that I'm all on my own
I saw you just the other day, my, how you have grown
Cast my memory back there, Lord
Sometime I'm overcome thinking 'bout
Making love in the green grass
Behind the stadium
With you, my brown eyed girl
With you, my brown eyed girl.
Do you remember when we used to sing:
Chorus

CALIFORNIA DREAMIN'

Words and Music by JOHN PHILLIPS
and MICHELLE PHILLIPS

E7
Am
G
To Coda
F
G
Bm7
Cal - i - for - nia dream-in'
On such a win - ter's day.
E7
Am
G
F
G
Bm7
Stopped in - to a church,
I passed a - long the way.
E7
F
C
E7
Am
F
E
Dm6
Oh, I got down on my knees,
And I pre - tend to pray.
E7
Am
G
F
G
Bm7
3
You know the preach-er likes the cold,
He knows I'm gon - na stay.

E7
Am
G
F
G
Cal - i - for - nia dream - in'
On such a win - ter's
Bm7
E7
D.S. al Coda
CODA
F
G
day.
All the leaves are
On such a win - ter's
Am
G
F
G
Am
G
F
G
day. (Cal - i - for - nia dream - in') On such a win - ter's day. (Cal - i - for - nia dream - in') On such a win - ter's
Fmaj7
Am
day.

CALIFORNIA GIRLS

Words and Music by BRIAN WILSON
and MIKE LOVE

Moderately
N.C.
p
Faster
B♭
rit.
mf
Well,
B♭
A♭/B♭
East Coast girls are hip, I real - ly dig those styles they wear;
West Coast has the sun - shine, and the girls all get so tanned;

Original key: B major. This edition has been transposed down one half-step to be more playable.

E♭
and the South - ern girls with the
I dig a French bi - ki - ni on Ha -
F7
way they talk they knock me out when I'm down there. The
wai - ian is - land dolls by a palm tree in the sand. I've
B♭
A♭/B♭
Mid - west farm - er's daugh - ters real - ly make you feel al - right.
been all a - round this great big world, and I've seen all kinds of girls.
E♭
And the North - ern girls with the
Yeah, but I could - n't wait to get

F7
way they kiss, they keep their boy - friends warm at night.
back in the States, back to the cut - est girls in the world.
B♭
Cm7
I wish they all could be Cal - i - for - nia, I
A♭
B♭m
G♭
wish they all could be Cal - i - for - nia, I wish they all could be
A♭m
1 B♭
Cal - i - for - nia girls.
The

2
B♭
L.H.
B♭
I wish they all could be Cal - i - for - nia, I
Cm7
Repeat and Fade
wish they all could be Cal - i - for - nia, I
Optional Ending
B♭
Cal - i - for - nia girls.

CRAZY

Words and Music by
WILLIE NELSON

E♭
Edim7
Fm7
B♭7
B♭7♯5
crazy for feel-in' so blue.
E♭
D♭
C
Fm
Fm(maj7)
I know you'd love me as long as you want-ed,
Fm7
B♭7
and then some-day you'd leave me for some-bod-y
E♭
A♭
E♭
E♭7
A♭
new. Wor-ry, why do I let my-self

Eb Ebmaj7 Eb6 Eb E F7
3fr
wor - ry, won - d'rin' what in the world did I
Bb7 Fm7 Bb7 Bb7#5 Eb Db C7
9fr
do? Cra - zy for think - ing that my love could
Fm Fm(maj7) Fm7 Ab Gm7
4fr
hold you. I'm cra - zy for try - in',
Fm7 Ebmaj7 Fm7 Bb7 Eb
cra - zy for cry - in' and I'm cra - zy for lov - in' you!

(Sittin' On)
THE DOCK OF THE BAY

Words and Music by STEVE CROPPER
and OTIS REDDING

Moderate beat

G

mp

G B

Sit - tin' in the morn - ing sun, I'll be
left my home in Geor - gia
Sit - tin' here rest - in' my bones, and this

C B B♭ A

sit - tin' when the eve - nin' come.
head - ed for the Fris - co bay.
lone - li - ness won't leave my a - lone.

G B

Watch - in' the ships roll in, then I
I have noth - in' to live for, look like
Two thou - sand miles I roam just to

C
B
B♭
A
watch 'em roll a - way a - gain.
noth - in's gon - na come my way.
make this dock my home.
Yeah, I'm
So I'm just gon'
Now I'm just gon'
G
Esus2
E
sit - tin' on the dock of the bay,
sit on the dock of the bay,
sit at the dock of the bay,
watch - in' the tide
G
Esus2
E
G
roll a - way.
Ooh, I'm just
sit - tin' on the dock of the bay,
A
G
To Coda
1 E
2 E
wast - in' time.
I

G
D
C
Looks like noth-in's gon-na change;
ev - 'ry-thing
still re-mains the same.
I can't do what ten peo-ple tell me to do,
F
so I guess I'll re-main the same.
D.S. al Coda
CODA
E
Repeat ad lib.
Optional Ending

A DAY IN THE LIFE

Words and Music by JOHN LENNON
and PAUL McCARTNEY

C
F
Em
Cmaj7
G
Bm/F♯
I saw the pho-to-graph
He blew his mind out in a
I saw a film to-day oh
Em
C
Em/B
Am
Cmaj7
car
boy
He did-n't no-tice that the lights had changed
The Eng-lish ar-my had just won the war
G
Bm
Em
C
F
A crowd of peo-ple stood and stared
A crowd of peo-ple turned a-way
They'd seen his face be-fore
But I just had to look
Em
Em/D
C
No-bod-y was real-ly sure if he was from the House of Lords.

2
Em
Em/D
C
Hav - ing read the book I'd
Bm/F♯
G
Em/A
love to turn you on.
E
Woke up,
D(no3rd)
fell out of bed, dragged a comb a-cross my head.
Found my

E
F♯m/B
E
F♯m/B
way down - stairs and drank a cup, and look-ing up I no-ticed I was late.
E
Found my coat and grabbed my hat made the bus in sec-onds
D(no3rd)
E
F♯m/B
B7
flat. Found my way up - stairs and had a smoke and
E
F♯m/B
C
G
some-bod-y spoke and I went in-to a dream. Ah

D
A
E
C
G
D
A
G
Bm/F#
I read the news to-day oh
Em
C
Em/B
boy
four thou-sand holes in Black-burn

Am Cmaj7 G Bm
Lan - ca-shire And though the holes were rath - er
Em C F
small They had to count them all
Em Em/D C
Now they know how man - y holes it takes to fill the Al - bert Hall I'd
Bm/F# G G/A E
love to turn you on.

DREAM ON

Words and Music by
STEVEN TYLER

Moderately slow
Fm
Cm/F
3fr
Fm6
B♭m6/F
Fm
C7sus/F
mp
Fm
Fm7
Fm6
B♭m6/F
Ev-'ry time ___ that I look in the mir - ror,
mf
Fm
Fm7
Fm6
B♭m6/F
all these lines on my face get-tin' clear - er.
Fm
Fm7
Fm6
B♭m6/F
The past ___ is gone; ___

Fm
Fm7
Fm6
B♭m6/F
it went by like dusk to dawn.
Dm7♭5
C
Dm7♭5
B♭m6/D♭
2fr
Is-n't that the way ev - 'ry-bod - y's got their dues in life to pay?
C
D♭maj7/C
D7/C
C7
Fm
E♭
3fr
I know no-bod - y knows
cresc.
f
D♭
E♭
3fr
Fm
E♭
3fr
where it comes and where it goes. I know it's ev - 'ry-bod - y's sin;

D♭
E♭
3fr
Fm
Fm7
you got to lose to know how to win.
mp
Fm6
B♭m6/F
Fm
Fm9
Fm
Fm
Fm7
Fm6
B♭m6/F
Fm
Fm7
Half my life's in books' writ-ten pag - es, lived and learned from
mf
Fm6
B♭m6/F
Fm
Fm7
fools and from sag - es. You know it's

Fm6
B♭m6/F
Fm
Fm7
true,
all these things
cresc.
Fm6
B♭m6/F
Fm
E♭
3fr
come back to you.
Sing with me, sing for the years,
f
D♭
E♭
3fr
Fm
E♭
3fr
sing for the laugh-ter 'n' sing for the tears.
Sing with me if it's just for to-day,
Dm7♭5
D♭maj7
B♭m/C
C
B♭m/C
C
B♭m/C
C
B♭m/C
C
may-be to-mor-row the good Lord will take you a-way.

B♭m/C
C
B♭
D♭
E♭
3fr
Fm
Dream on,
dream on,
dream on,
dream your-self a dream come true.
Dream on,
dream on,
dream on
and dream un-til your dream comes true.
ff

Bb
C
Dream on, dream on,
Db
Eb
3fr
Fm
G
8va
dream on, dream on.
Dream on, dream on,
Ab
4fr
Bb
Bbm/C
C
(8va)
dream on, ah.
Ah.
Fm
Eb
3fr
loco
Sing with me, sing for the years,

Db
Eb
Fm
Eb
sing for the laugh - ter-'n' sing for the tears.
Sing with me if it's just for to - day,
1
Db
Eb
may-be to-mor - row the good Lord will take you a-way.
2
Dm7b5
Db
may-be to-mor - row the good Lord will take you a -
Bbm/C
C
way.
Repeat and Fade
mf

EVERY BREATH YOU TAKE

Written and Composed by
G.M. SUMNER

C
D
Dsus
ev - 'ry bond you break, ev - 'ry step you take, I'll be watch-ing you.
Em
D7sus
G
Ev - 'ry sin - gle day,
Em
ev - 'ry word you say, ev - 'ry game you play,
C
D
Dsus
G
ev - 'ry night you stay, I'll be watch-ing you.

C
C/B♭
Am7
Oh, can't you see you be - long to
G
A7
me? How my poor heart aches
D
D7sus
with ev - 'ry step you take. Ev - 'ry move you
G
Em
make, ev - 'ry vow you break,

C
D
Dsus
ev - 'ry smile _ you fake, ev - 'ry claim _ you stake, I'll be watch-ing you.
Em
To Coda
E♭
3 fr
Since you've gone, _ I been lost _
_ with - out _ a trace,
F
I dream at night I can on - ly see _ your face.
E♭
3 fr
I look a-round, but it's you I can't _ re-place.
F
I feel so cold and I

E♭
3 fr
long for your em-brace. I keep cry - ing, ba - by, ba - by, please
G
Em
C
D
1
Em
D

2
G
D.S. al Coda
Oh, can't you
CODA
Em
C
Ev - 'ry move you make, ev - 'ry step you take,
D
Dsus
I'll be watch-ing you.
D7sus
I'll be watch - ing

G
Em
you. Ev - 'ry breath take, ev - 'ry move you make, ev - 'ry bond you break,
you. (Ev - 'ry move you make, ev - 'ry vow you break, ev - 'ry smile you fake,
C
G
ev - 'ry step you take, ev - 'ry sin - gle day,
ev - 'ry claim you stake,
I'll be watch - ing you.
Em
ev - 'ry word you say, ev - 'ry game you play,
Repeat and Fade
Optional Ending
C
C
G
ev - 'ry night you stay.) I'll be watch - ing you.
I'll be watch - ing

FIRE AND RAIN

Words and Music by
JAMES TAYLOR

C
Gm7
F
C
I walked out this morn - ing and I wrote down this song
My bod - y's ach - ing and my time is at hand
G
B♭maj7
I just can't re - mem - ber who to send it to.
And I won't make it an - y oth - er way.
Chorus:
F
F/E
Dm7
G7
C
I've seen fire and I've seen rain I've seen

F
F/E
Dm7
G7
C
sun - ny days that I thought would nev - er end
I've seen
F
F/E
Dm7
G7
C
lone - ly times when I could not find a friend
But I
B♭
F/A
Gm7
C9
al - ways thought that I'd see you a - gain.
1,2
2nd time to Verse 3
2. Won't you
3. Now I'm
Fine

Verse 3:
C
Gm7/C
F/C
C
walk - ing my mind to an eas - y time my back turned towards the sun
G/C
3fr
B♭/C
Lord knows when the cold wind blows it - 'll turn your head a - round Well, there's
C
Gm7/C
F/C
C
hours of time on the tel - e - phone line to talk a - bout things to come
G/C
3fr
B♭/C
D.S. al Fine
Sweet dreams and fly - ing ma - chines in piec - es on the ground.

FOR WHAT IT'S WORTH

Words and Music by
STEPHEN STILLS

A
E
tell - in' me I've got to be - ware.
I think it's time we stop, chil - dren, what's that sound?
Ev - 'ry - bod - y look what's go - in' down.

A
E
A
E
A
1. There's bat - tle lines be - in' drawn, No - bod - y's
2. What a field day for the heat. A
3. Pa - ra - noi - a strikes deep,
E
A
right if ev - 'ry - bod - y's wrong,
thou - sand peo - ple in the street sing - in'
in - to your life it will creep. It

E
A
Young peo - ple speak - in' their minds,
songs and car - ry - in' signs.
starts when you're al - ways a - fraid.
Get - tin'
Most - ly
Step out of
To Coda
so much re - sis - tance from be - hind. I think it's time we
say - ing, "Hoo - ray for our side."
line the men come and
stop, chil - dren, what's that sound? Ev - 'ry - bod - y look what's go - in' down.

E
A
E
A
After repeat
D.S. al Coda
Coda
A
E
take you a - way. You bet - ter
E
A
Repeat and fade
stop, hey, what's that sound? Ev - 'ry-bod - y look what's go - in'down. You bet - ter

GLORIA

Words and Music by
VAN MORRISON

C Bb F C Bb F C Bb F C Bb F
night. She makes me feel so good Lord, makes me feel al -
house. She knocks up - on my door, makes me feel al -
right. Her name is G l
right.
o r i a
G l o r i a
Glo - ri - a
G l o r i

C
B♭
F
a
G l o r i a
a
Glo - ri - a
Glo - ri -
Al - right one time.
a
Glo - ri - a
Glo - ri -
a.
1 C
2 C
Yeah, she comes a - round

FREE BIRD

Words and Music by ALLEN COLLINS
and RONNIE VAN ZANT

Slowly
mf
G
D/F#
Em
If I leave here to - mor - row,
Bye, bye ba - by, it's been a sweet love
F
C
D
Would you still re - mem - ber me?
though this feel - ing I can't change.

G
D/F#
Em
For I must be trav - 'ling on now
But please don't take it so bad - ly
F
C
D
'cause there's too man - y plac - es I've got to see.
'cause the Lord knows I'm to blame.
G
D/F#
Em
But if I stayed here with you, girl,
F
C
D
things just could - n't be the same.

G
D/F#
Em
'Cause I'm as free as a bird now,
F
C
Dsus
D
Dsus
D
And this bird you'll nev - er change,
F
C
D
And this bird you can - not change,
F
C
D
And this bird you can - not change.

F
C
D
To Coda
Lord knows I can't change.
G
D/F#
Em
(Instrumental)
F
C
1 D
2 D
D.C. al Coda
CODA
F
C
D
Lord, help me, I can't change.

GIMME SOME LOVIN'

Words and Music by STEVE WINWOOD, MUFF WINWOOD and SPENCER DAVIS

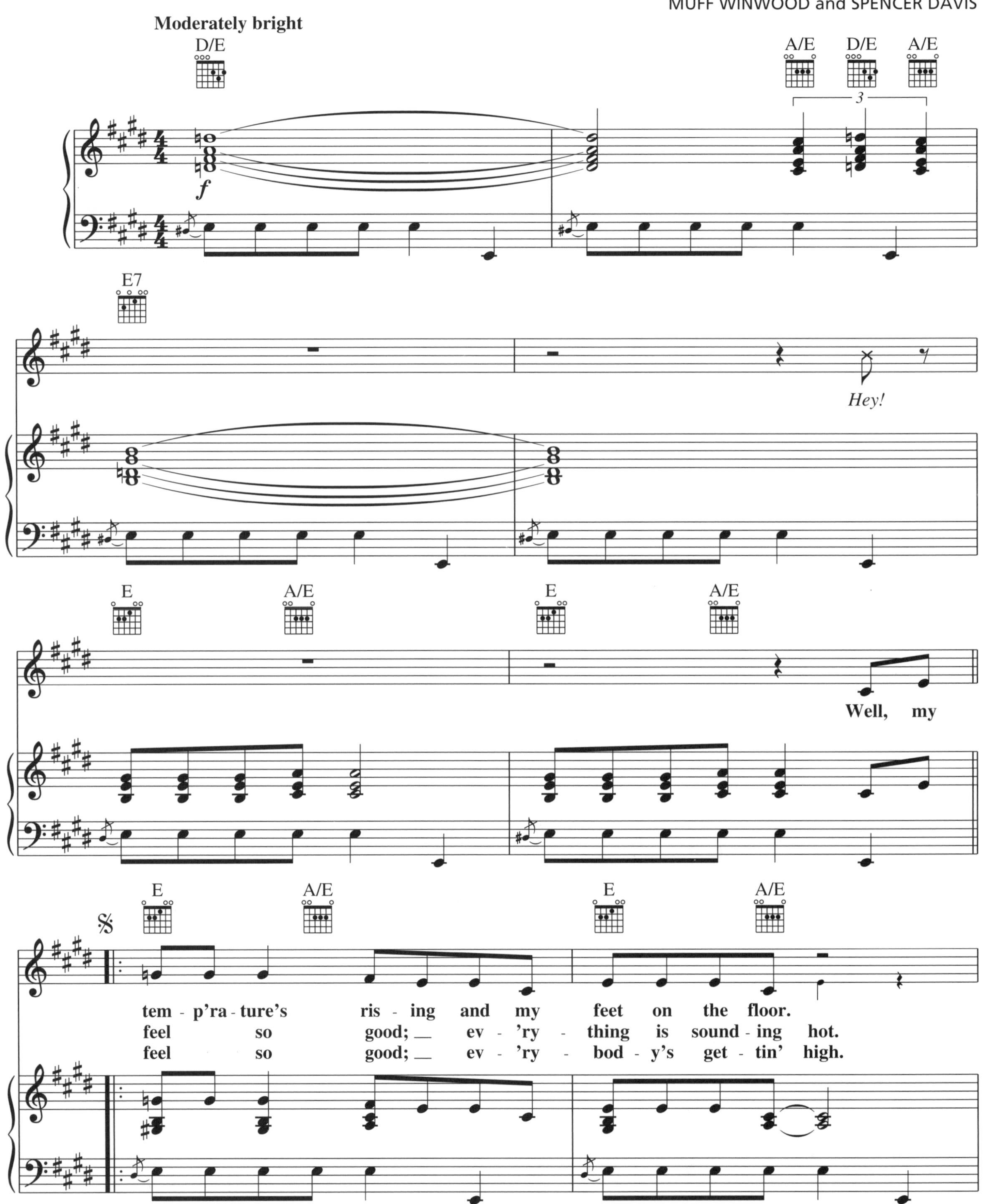

E
A/E
E
A/E
Twen - ty peo - ple knock - in' 'cause they're want - ing some more.
Bet - ter take it eas - y, 'cause the place is on fire.
Bet - ter take it eas - y, 'cause the place is on fire.
E
A/E
E
A/E
Let me in, ba - by, I don't know what you've got. But you'd
Been a hard day and I don't know what to do.
Been a hard day, noth - in' went too good. Now I'm
E
A/E
E
A/E
bet - ter take it eas - y. This place is hot.
Wait a min - ute, ba - by. It could hap - pen to you.
gon - na re - lax, hon - ey. Ev - 'ry - bod - y should.
E
G
So glad we made it,

A
C
E
A/E
so glad _ we made _ it. You got - ta gim - me some
E
A/E
To Coda
lov - in', gim - me some lov - in',
E
A/E
E
gim - me some lov - in' ev - er - y day.
D/E
A/E
D/E
A/E
3

E7
E
A/E
Hey!
1 E
A/E
2 E
A/E
D.S. al Coda
Well, I
Well, I
CODA
E
A/E
gim - me some lov - in,'
E
A/E
Repeat and Fade
gim - me some lov - in,'

GOD ONLY KNOWS

Words and Music by BRIAN WILSON
and TONY ASHER

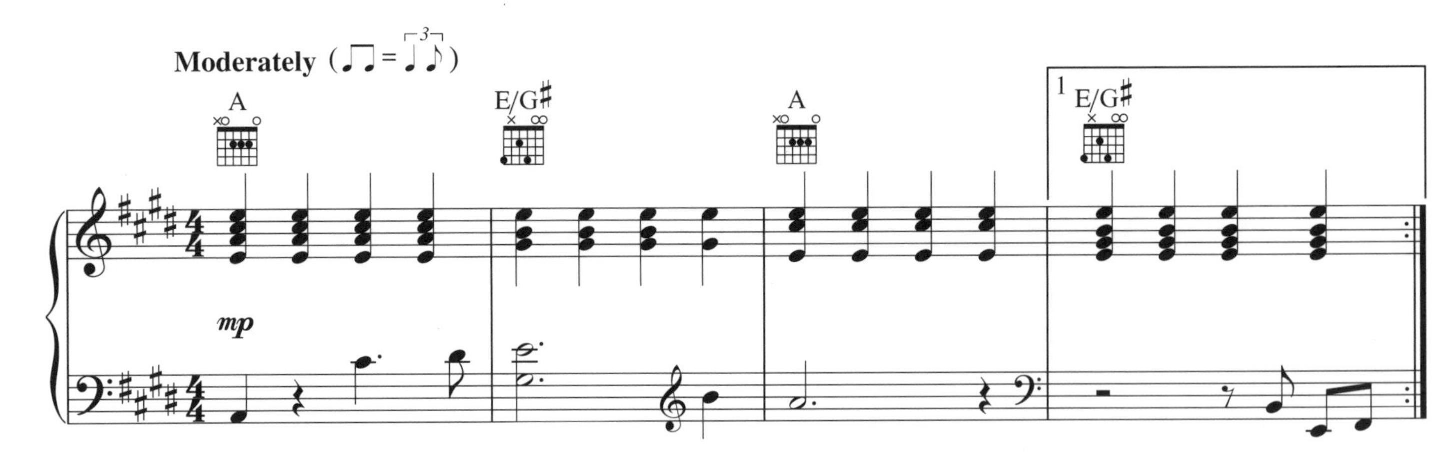
Moderately
A
E/G♯
A
1 E/G♯
mp

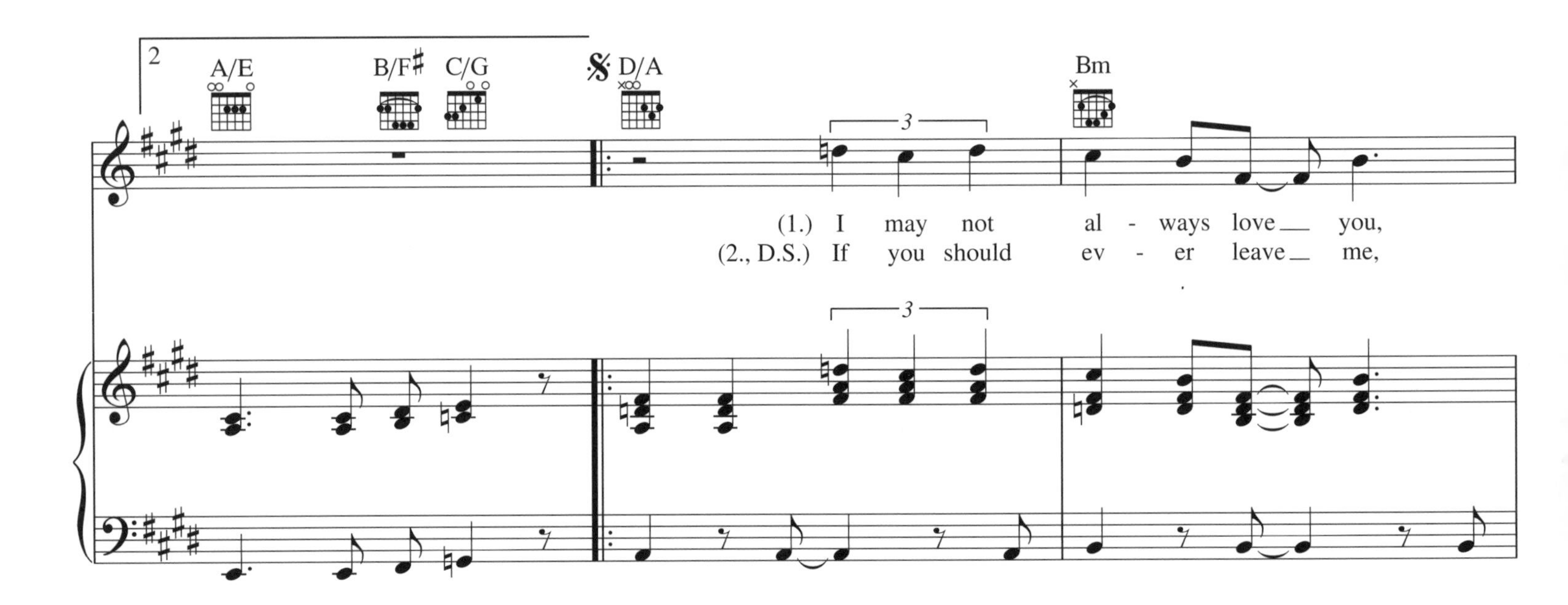
2 A/E
B/F♯
C/G
D/A
Bm
(1.) I may not al - ways love you,
(2., D.S.) If you should ev - er leave me,

F♯m
B7/A
but long as there are stars a - bove you,
well, life would still go on, be - lieve me.

E/B
A6/C♯
E/B
you'll nev - er need to doubt it. I'll make you so
The world could show noth - ing to me, so what good would
F♯9
A
E/G♯
sure a - bout it.
liv - ing do me?
God on - ly knows what I'd be with - out
F♯m7
To Coda
E
N.C.
N.C.
you.
G/D
Em6
Oo, oo.

Bm/F♯
Bm7
E/D
A/E
Oo,
oo.
Oo,
(Do, do, do, do, do, do, do. Do, do, do, do. Do, do, do,
(Ba, ba, ba, ba, ba, ba, ba, ba, ba.
G♯dim7/F
A/E
D♯m7♭5
6fr
oo,
oo.
do, do, do, do, do, do, do. Do, do, do, do.)
Ba, ba, ba, ba, ba, ba, ba, ba, ba, ba, ba, oo.)
D
A/C♯
Bm7
D.S. al Coda
3
And God on - ly knows what I'd be with - out you.

CODA
E/G♯
A
E/G♯
God on - ly knows what I'd be with - out

F♯m7
E/G♯
A
Repeat and Fade
you.
(God on - ly knows what I'd be with - out
God on - ly knows
you.)

Optional Ending
E/G♯
F♯m7
E
what I'd be with - out
you.

GOOD GOLLY MISS MOLLY

Words and Music by ROBERT BLACKWELL
and JOHN MARSCALCO

Moderate rock tempo
F7
mf
C7#5
F7
Good gol - ly Miss Mol - ly,
yeah, you sure like a ball.
Well, good gol - ly Miss
B♭7
Mol - ly,
yeah, you sure like a ball.

F7
When you're shak - in' and a -
C7
Bb7
F7
shout - in', can't you hear_ your mom-ma call?
C7#5
F
Bb7
F
Bb7
Well, from the ear - ly, ear - ly morn-in' to the ear - ly, ear - ly night, when I
mom-ma, pop-pa told me, "Son, you'd bet-ter watch your step." What I
F
no chord
F
no chord
F
caught Miss Mol - ly rock - in' at the House of Blue Lights._ Ooh! Good gol - ly Miss
knew a - bout Miss Mol - ly, got - ta watch my dad-dy my - self. Good gol - ly Miss

B♭7
F7
Mol - ly, yeah, you sure like a ball.
Mol - ly, yeah, you sure like a ball.
C7
When you're rock - in' and a - roll - in',
When you're shak - in' and a - shout - in',
B♭7
1 F7
can't you hear your mom - ma call?
can't you hear your mom - ma
C7♯5
2 F7
E♭
F
Well, now call?
3
3

GOOD VIBRATIONS

Words and Music by BRIAN WILSON
and MIKE LOVE

Original key: E♭ minor. This edition has been transposed down one half-step to be more playable.

C6
hear the sound of a gen - tle word on the
I look in her eyes she goes
B♭
A
wind that lifts her per - fume through the air.
with me to a blos - som world.
C7
F
B♭/F
F
B♭/F
cresc.
I'm think - in' of good vi - bra - tions.
F
B♭/F
F
B♭/F
F
B♭/F
She's giv - in' me the ex - ci - ta - tions. Ooh bop bop,
I'm pick - in' up

F7
B♭/F
F
B♭/F
F7
B♭/F
good_ vi - bra - tions, bop bop. Ex - ci - ta -
good vi - bra - tions. She's giv - in' me the ex - ci - ta - tions.
G
C/G
G7
C/G
G
C/G
Good, good, good, good_ vi - bra - tions._______
- tions bop bop. Good_ vi - bra - tions bop bop.
I'm pick - in' up good vi - bra - tions. She' giv - in' me the
G7
C/G
A
D/A
A7
D/A
Good, good, good, good_ vi - bra -
Ex - ci - ta - tions bop bop. Good_ vi - bra -
ex - ci - ta - tions. I'm pick - in' up good vi - bra - tions.

A
D/A
A7
D/A
Dm
tions.
tions, bop bop. Ex - ci - ta - tions.
She's giv - in' me the ex - ci - ta - tions. Close my eyes.
A
D/A
A7
D/A
tions.
She's some - how - tions bop bop. Ex - ci -
She's giv - in' me the ex - ci - ta - tions.
Em/A
D/A
A
D/A
Em/A
D/A
A
D/A
Em/A
D/A
ta - tions.
mp

A D/A Em/A D/A A D/A Em/A D/A A D/A
Ah
Em/A D/A A D/A Am/D G/D
I don't know where, but she sends
my my, what e - la - tion.
D G/D Am/E G/D D G/D
me there. My my, one sen - sa -
Em/A D/A A D/A Em/A D/A A7 D/A
Oh, my, my, what e - la - tion.
- tion. Ah, my, my, one...

Suddenly Slower

E
F♯m
B7
p
E
F♯m
Got - ta keep those lov - in' good vi - bra - tions a -
B7
E
hap - 'nin' with her. Got - ta keep those lov - in' good
F♯m
B7
E
Vocal fades out
vi - bra - tions a - hap - 'nin' with her. Got - ta keep

F♯m
B7
those lov - in' good vi - bra - tions a - hap - 'nin' with her.
E
F♯m
B7
E
D/E
Ah.
Tempo I
A
D/A
A7
D/A
A
D/A
Good, good, good, good vi - bra - tions.
Ooh bop bop good vi - bra - tions bop bop.
I'm pick - in' up good vi - bra - tions. She's giv - in' me the

A7
D/A
G
C/G
G7
C/G
Good, good, good, good vi - bra -
Ex - ci - ta - tions bop bop. Good vi - bra -
ex - ci - ta - tions. Good good good.
3
G
C/G
G7
C/G
N.C.
- tions.
- tions.
3
3
8vb
F
G
Na na na na na na na na. Na na na na na
Ba ba ba ba ba
(8vb)

A
G
Do, do, do, do, do, do, do, do. Do, do, do, do,
na na na. Na na na na na na na na Na na na na na
ba. Ba ba ba ba ba ba. Da da da da da
(8vb)
N.C.
G
C/G
do, do, do, do.
na na na.
da.
Repeat and Fade
Optional Ending
G7
C/G
G
C/G
G7
C/G

GREAT BALLS OF FIRE

Words and Music by OTIS BLACKWELL
and JACK HAMMER

G7
F7
me, hon-ey.
I changed my mind,
love's just fine.
C
no chord
Good - ness gra - cious, great balls of fire!
Instrumental ends
Kiss me, ba - by.
Woo,
it feels good.
Hold me, ba - by.
Girl, just let me love you like a lov - er should.
I want to love you like a lov - er should.
You're fine,

so kind, I'm gon-na tell the world that you're mine, mine, mine, mine.
C
F7
I chew my nails and I twid-dle my thumb. I'm real ner-vous but it
G7
F7
1 C
no chord
sure is fun. Come on, ba-by, you're driv-ing me cra-zy. Good-ness gra-cious, great
2 C
no chord
C
balls of fire! Good-ness gra-cious, great balls of fire!

A HARD DAY'S NIGHT

C
D
get home to you I find the thing that you do will make me
love to come home 'Cause when I get you a - lone you know I'll
G
C9
To Coda
G
G
Bm
feel al - right. You know I
be O. K. When I'm home
Em
Bm
G
ev - 'ry - thing seems to be al - right. When I'm home
Em
C
D
feel - ing you hold - ing me tight, tight, yeah, It's been a

G
C(add9)
G
F6
hard day's night
and I've been work - ing like a
dog.
It's been a hard day's night
I should be
sleep - ing like a log.
But when I get home to you
I find the
C
D
thing that you do will make me feel al - right.
C9

G
C7
G
F6
G
C7
G
F6
G
So why I
C
D
love to come home 'Cause when I get you a - lone you know I
G
C9
G
Bm
feel O. K. When I'm home

Em
Bm
G
ev - 'ry - thing seems to be al - right.
When I'm home
Em
C
D
D.S. al Coda
feel - ing you hold - ing me tight,
tight, yeah, It's been a
CODA
G
C9
G
You know I feel al - right,
You know I
C(add9)
F(add9)
Repeat and Fade
feel al - right.

HEARTBREAK HOTEL

Words and Music by MAE BOREN AXTON,
TOMMY DURDEN and ELVIS PRESLEY

E7
N.C.
E7
(D.S.) though it's al - ways crowd - ed, you still can find some room for
bell - hop's tears keep flow - ing and the desk - clerk's dressed in black. Well, they
N.C.
E7
bro - ken - heart - ed lov - ers to cry there in the gloom. You'll be so,
been so long on Lone - ly Street they'll nev - er, nev - er look back. It'll make you so,
A7
B7
To Coda
it'll make you so lone - ly, ba - by. It'll make you so lone - ly. Oh, they're so lone - ly they could
it'll make you so lone - ly, ba - by. Well, they're so lone - ly. Oh, they're so lone - ly they could
1
E
2
E
E7
die. Now the die. Well, now if your ba - by leaves you and you've
Instrumental solo

N.C.
E7
got a tale to tell, well, just take a walk down Lone - ly Street to
E7
A7
Heart - break Ho - tel where you will be, you will be so lone - ly, ba - by.
B7
1
E
Well, you'll be lone - ly. You'll be so lone - ly you could die.
2
E
D.S. al Coda
Solo ends
Al -
CODA
die.
F7

HOTEL CALIFORNIA

Words and Music by DON HENLEY, GLENN FREY and DON FELDER

1
2
Bm
On a dark des - ert
Her mind is Tif - fa - ny
mf
F♯7
high - way, cool wind in my hair,
twist - ed. She got the Mer - ce - des bends.
A
E7
warm smell of co - li - tas ris - ing up through the
She got a lot of pret - ty, pret - ty boys she calls
G
air. Up a - head in the dis - tance,
friends. How they dance in the court - yard;

D
Em7
I saw a shim - mer - ing light. My head grew heav - y and my
sweet sum - mer sweat. Some dance to re -
F#7
sight grew dim; I had to stop for the night.
mem - ber; some dance to for - get.
Bm
F#7
There she stood in the door - way; I heard the mis - sion bell.
So I called up the cap - tain: "Please bring me my
A
And I was think - ing to my - self: this could be
wine." He said, "We have - n't had that spir - it here since

E7
G
heav - en or this could be hell.
nine - teen six - ty - nine."
Then she lit up a
And still those
D
can - dle, and she showed me the way.
voic - es are call - ing from far a - way;
Em7
There were voic - es down the cor - ri - dor;
wake you up in the mid - dle of the night
F♯7
I thought I heard them say:
just to hear them say:

G
"Wel - come to the Ho - tel Cal - i - for -
"Wel - come to the Ho - tel Cal - i - for -
D
F#7
- nia. Such a love - ly place, (such a
- nia. Such a love - ly place, (such a
Bm
love - ly place) such a love - ly face.
love - ly place) such a love - ly face. They
G
D
Plen - ty of room at the Ho - tel Cal - i - for - nia.
liv - in' it up at the Ho - tel Cal - i - for - nia.

Em7
An - y time of year, (an - y time of year) you can
What a nice sur - prise; (what a nice sur - prise) bring your
1 F♯7
find it here."
2 F♯7
al - i - bis."
N.C.
Bm
Mir - rors on the ceil - ing,
Last thing I re - mem - ber, I was
Guitar Solo ad lib.
F♯7
the pink cham - pagne on ice, and she said,
run - ning for the door.
A
"We are all just
I had to find the

E7
pris - on - ers here of our own de - vice."
pas - sage back to the place I was be - fore.
G
D
And in the mas - ter's cham - bers, they gath - ered for the
"Re - lax," said the night man. "We are pro - grammed to re -
feast.
ceive.
Em7
They stab it with their steel - y knives, but they
You can check out an - y time you like, but
F♯7
just can't kill the beast.
you can nev - er leave."
Repeat ad lib. and Fade
Optional Ending
Bm

HEY JUDE

Words and Music by JOHN LENNON
and PAUL McCARTNEY

C7
F
to make it bet - ter.
Hey
F
C
C7
C7sus
C7
Jude, don't be a - fraid.
You were made to go out and
Jude, don't let me down.
You have found her, now go and
F
B♭
get her.
The min - ute you let her un - der your
get her.
Re - mem - ber to let her in - to your
F
C7
F
skin, then you be - gin to make it bet - ter.
heart; then you can start to make it bet - ter.

F7
Bb
Bb/A
And any - time you feel the pain, hey Jude, re - frain;
So let it out and let it in. Hey Jude, be - gin;
Gm7
3 fr
Gm7/F
C7/E
C7
F
don't car - ry the world up - on your shoul - ders.
you're wait - ing for some - one to per - form with.
F7
Bb
Bb/A
For well you know that it's a fool who plays it cool
And don't you know that it's just you? Hey Jude, you'll do.
Gm7
3 fr
Gm7/F
C7/E
C7
by mak - ing his world a lit - tle cold -
The move - ment you need is on your shoul -

F
F7
C7
er.
der.
Da da da da da da da da da.
1
2
D.S. al Coda
Hey
Hey Jude,
CODA
C7
to make it bet -
F
ter, bet - ter, bet - ter, bet - ter, bet - ter, bet - ter, oh.
F
Da da da
E♭
3 fr
B♭
F
Repeat and Fade
Optional Ending
da da da da,
da da da da,
hey Jude.

HOUND DOG

Words and Music by JERRY LEIBER
and MIKE STOLLER

G7
F7
C
nev - er caught a rab - bit and you ain't no friend of mine.
C
Well, they said you was high - classed,
but, that was just a
lie.
F7
Yeah, they said you was high - classed,
C
but, that was just a lie.
Yeah, you ain't

G7
F7
C
nev - er caught a rab - bit and you ain't no friend of mine.
1.2.
3.
D.S. al Coda
You ain't noth - in' but a
You ain't noth - in' but a
Coda
G7
F7
nev - er caught a rab - bit, and you ain't no friend of mine.
C
C7

I GOT YOU
(I Feel Good)

Words and Music by
JAMES BROWN

D7
I knew that I would now.
Ah, sug - ar and spice.
So good
So nice
A7
G7
1 D9
To Coda
so good, I got you.
so nice, I got you.
Woh!
I feel nice.
2 D9
no chord

G7
When I hold you in my arms I
D7
know that I can do no wrong. and
G7
A7
when I hold you in my arms my
love won't do you no harm.
love can't do me no harm.
D7
And I feel nice. Ah, sug - ar and spice.

G7
I feel nice.
D7
Ah, sug - ar and spice.
So nice,
A7
G7
so nice,
I got you.
1 D9
2 D9
D.S. al Coda
Woh! I feel good.

CODA
D9
A7
So good, so good,
G7
D9
'cause I got you.
So good,
A7
G7
D9
so good, 'cause I got you.
Hey!
rit.

I HEARD IT THROUGH THE GRAPEVINE

Words and Music by NORMAN J. WHITFIELD
and BARRETT STRONG

Moderately
N.C.
Em
A/E
Em
A/E
Em
A/E
Em
Mm. I
bet you're won - derin' how I knew
ain't sup - posed to cry,
of what you see,
B
A7
'bout your plans to make me blue, with some oth - er guy
but these tears I can't hold in - side. Los - in' you
son, and none of what you hear. But I can't help

Em
B
A7
you knew be-fore. Be-tween the two of us guys you know I loved you more.
would end my life you see, 'cause you mean that much to me.
but be con-fused. If it's true, please tell me dear.
C♯m
4 fr
A7
It took me by sur - prise I must say when I
You could have told me your - self that you
Do you plan to let me go for the o - ther
Em
A7
Em
A7
Em
found out yes - ter - day. Don't you know that I heard it through the grape - vine,
loved some - one else. In - stead I heard it through the grape - vine,
guy you loved be - fore? Don't you know that I heard it through the grape - vine,
A
Em
not much lon - ger would you be mine. Oh, I heard
not much lon - ger would you be mine. Oh, I heard
not much lon - ger would you be mine. Oh, I heard

A7
Em
it through the grape - vine. Oh, I'm just
it through the grape - vine. And I'm just
it through the grape - vine. Oh, I'm just
A7
a - bout to lose my mind.
a - bout to lose my mind.
a - bout to lose my mind.
Hon - ey, hon - ey, oh
(I
Em
yeah.
heard it through the grape - vine, not much lon - ger would you be mine, ba -
- by.)
To Coda
1
2
Ooh. I know a man
Ooh.
Yeah,
Ooh.

D.S. al Coda
People say believe half
CODA
yeah, yeah, yeah. I heard it through the grape-vine, not much
longer would you be mine, ba - by. Yeah,
Repeat and Fade

I WANT TO HOLD YOUR HAND

Words and Music by JOHN LENNON
and PAUL McCARTNEY

Em
Bm
C
D
I want to hold your hand,
you'll let me hold your hand,
I want to hold your
Now let me hold your
G
Em
C
D
1 G
hand,
hand,
I want to hold your hand.
I want to hold your
Oh,
2 G
Dm7
G
hand.
And when I touch you I feel
more smoothly
C
Am
Dm7
hap - py in - side.
It's such a

G
C
D
C
D
feel - ing that my love I can't hide, I can't hide,
C
D
I can't hide!
G
D
Yeah, you got that some - thing
Yeah, you got that some - thing
as before
Em
Bm
G
I think you'll un - der - stand. When I say that
I think you'll un - der - stand. When I feel that

D
Em
Bm
some - thing,
some - thing,
I want to hold your hand,
C
D
G
Em
1 C
D
I want to hold your hand,
I want to hold your
G
2 C
D
B7
hand.
I want to hold your hand,
C
D
C
G
I want to hold your hand.

IMAGINE

Words and Music by
JOHN LENNON

Am/E
Dm7
F/C
G
C/G
I-mag-ine all the peo - ple living for to - day.
G7
C
Cmaj7
F
Ah. I-mag-ine there's no coun - tries.
sions.
C
Cmaj7
F
It is - n't hard to do.
I won-der if you can.
C
Cmaj7
F
Noth-ing to kill or die for,
No need for greed or hun - ger,

C
Cmaj7
F
and no re - li - gion, too.
a broth - er - hood of man.
Am/E
Dm7
F/C
G
C/G
I-mag - ine all the peo - ple liv - ing life in peace.
I-mag - ine all the peo - ple shar - ing all the world.
G7
F
G
You, you may say I'm a
C
E7
F
G
dream - er, but I'm not the on - ly one.

C
E7
F
G
I hope some - day you'll
join us
1
and the world will
be as one.
Cmaj7
I - mag - ine no pos - ses -
2
and the world will live as one.
rit.

IN THE MIDNIGHT HOUR

Words and Music by STEVE CROPPER
and WILSON PICKETT

A♭ B♭ A♭
hold you, and do all the things I told you in the mid-night
E♭ A♭ E♭ A♭ E♭ A♭ D♭ B♭
hour. Yes, I am, oh yes, I am.
E♭ A♭ E♭ A♭
I'm gon - na wait 'til stars come out and see that
E♭ A♭ E♭ A♭ E♭ A♭ E♭ A♭
twin - kle in your eyes. I'm gon - na wait 'til the mid-night hour, that's when my

Eb
6fr
Ab
4fr
Bb
Bb7
love begins to shine.
You'll be the only girl I'll love,
and
really love you
so in the midnight
hour,
oh
yeah, in the midnight
1
2
hour.
I'm gonna
hour.
I'm gonna
Optional Ending
Repeat and Fade
wait 'til the midnight
hour.
I'm gonna
wait 'til the midnight
hour.
rit.

JAILHOUSE ROCK

from SMOKEY JOE'S CAFE

Words and Music by JERRY LEIBER
and MIKE STOLLER

Moderately
D7
E♭7
mf
1. The
war - den threw a par - ty in the
2.-5. (See additional lyrics)
coun - ty jail.
The
pris - on band was there and they be -
gan to wail.
The
band was jump - in' and the joint be -

D7
Eb7
Chorus
gan to swing. You should have heard those knocked - out jail - birds sing. Let's
Ab7
4fr
Eb7
rock! Ev - 'ry - bod - y let's rock!
To Coda
Bb7
Ab7
4fr
Ev - 'ry - bod - y in the whole cell block was danc -
1-3
Eb7
D7
4
Eb7
- ing to the Jail - house Rock! - ing to the Jail - house

Additional Lyrics

2. Spider Murphy played the tenor saxophone
   Little Joe was blowin' on the slide trombone.
   The drummer boy from Illinois went crash, boom, bang;
   The whole rhythm section was the Purple Gang.
   (Chorus)

3. Number Forty-seven said to number Three:
   "You're the cutest jailbird I ever did see.
   I sure would be delighted with your company,
   Come on and do the Jailhouse Rock with me."
   (Chorus)

4. The sad sack was a-sittin' on a block of stone,
   Way over in the corner weeping all alone.
   The warden said: "Hey, Buddy, don't you be no square,
   If you can't find a partner, use a wooden chair!"
   (Chorus)

5. Shifty Henry said to Bugs: "For heaven's sake,
   No one's lookin', now's our chance to make a break."
   Bugsy turned to Shifty and he said: "Nix, nix;
   I wanna stick around a while and get my kicks."
   (Chorus)

JOHNNY B. GOODE

Words and Music by
CHUCK BERRY

F
write so well, But he could play a gui - tar just like a - ring - in' a bell.
stop and say Oh my, but that lit - tle coun - try boy could play.
lights A - say - in' John - ny B. Goode to - night."
Go! Go!
mf
F6
F7
Go! John - ny! Go! Go!
Go! John - ny! Go! Go!
Bb9
F6
C7
Go! John - ny! Go! Go!
Go! John - ny! Go! Go!
1,2
3
C7+5
F
Gb7
John - ny B. Goode.
2. He used to
3. His
mp

JUMP

Words and Music by EDWARD VAN HALEN, ALEX VAN HALEN,
MICHAEL ANTHONY and DAVID LEE ROTH

F/C
C
F/C
C/F
Gsus
3fr
G/C
C
I get up,
and noth-ing gets me
down.
You got it tough.
I seen the tough-est soul a-round.
And I

G/C
C
F/C
G/C
C
F/C
know,
ba-by, just how you
feel.
C/F
Gsus
G/C
C
F/C
G/C
You got to
roll
with the
punch-es
to get to what's
C
F/C
C/F
Gsus
Am
real.
Ah, can't you
see me stand-ing here? I got my
back a-gainst the rec-ord ma-chine.
F
C/E
Dm
I ain't the worst that you've seen.

F
C/E
Dm
G
Ah, can't you see what I mean?
G/C
C
3fr
Ah, might as well jump.
F/C
C/F
Gsus
To Coda
Might as well jump.
Go a-head and jump.
Go a-head and jump.
Might as well jump.
Go a-head and jump.

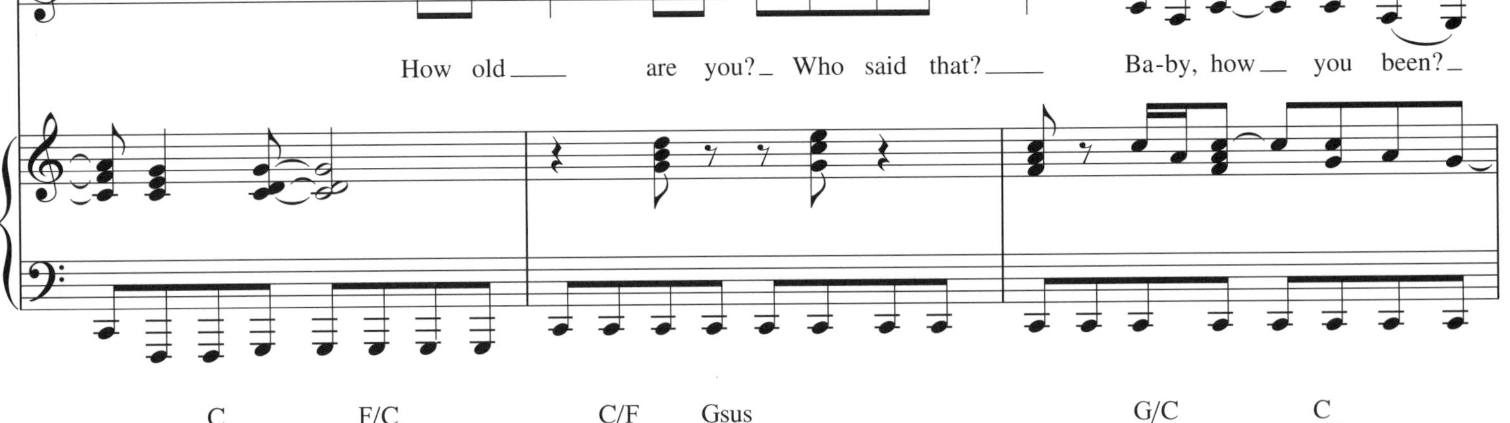
C/F
Gsus
G/C
C
F/C
G/C
3fr
How old are you? Who said that? Ba-by, how you been?

C
F/C
C/F
Gsus
G/C
C
3fr
You say you don't know. You won't

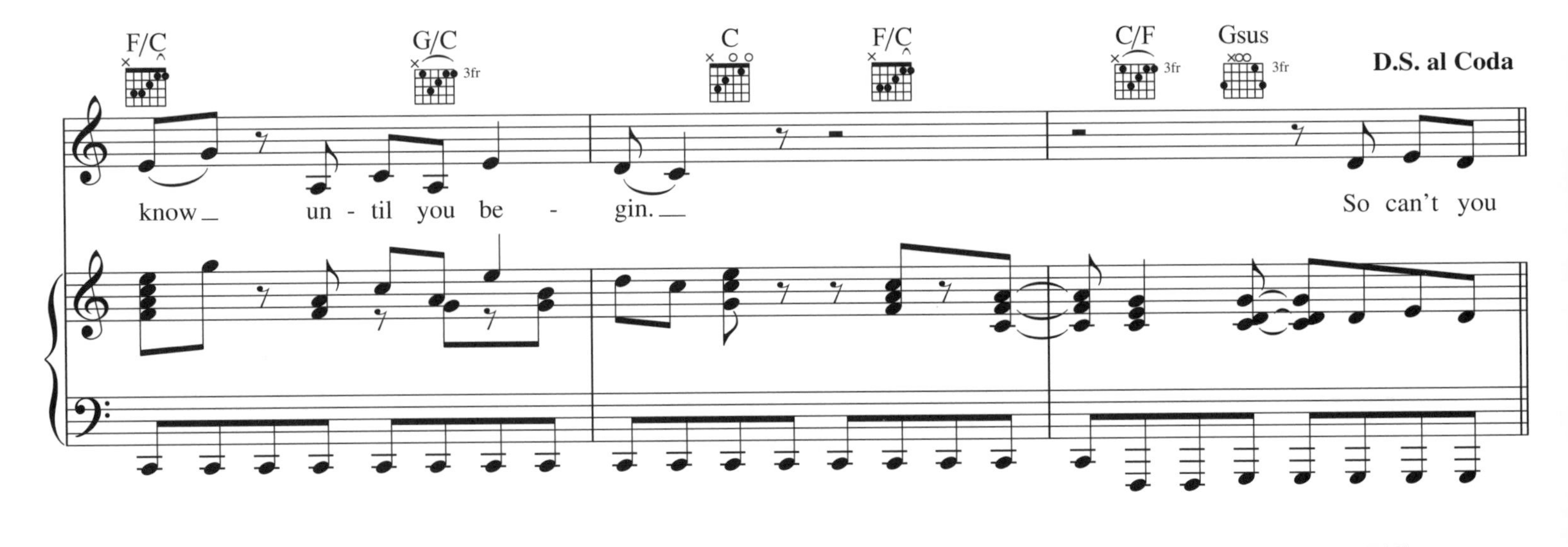
F/C
G/C
C
F/C
C/F
Gsus
3fr
D.S. al Coda
know until you be - gin. So can't you

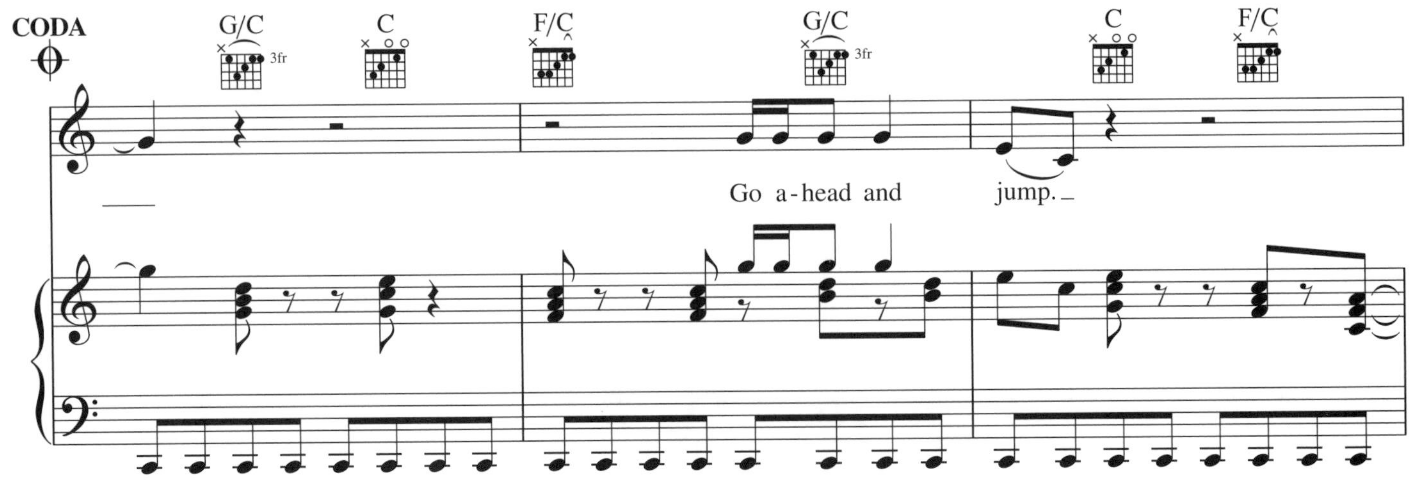
CODA
G/C
C
F/C
G/C
C
F/C
3fr
Go a-head and jump.

C/F
Gsus
3fr
B♭m
G♭
A♭
4fr
D♭
Jump!
G/C
C
F/C
G/F
F

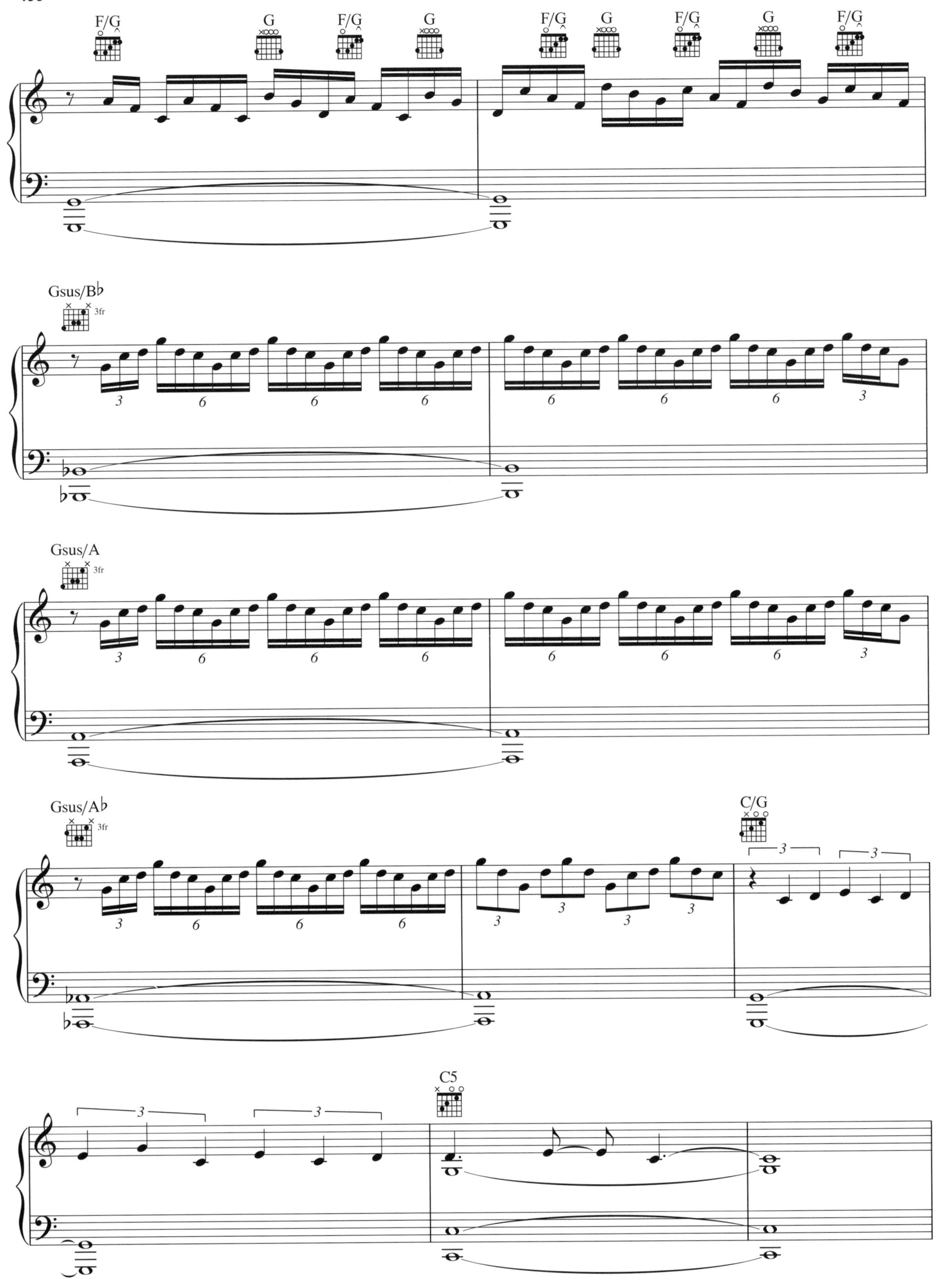
F/G
G
F/G
G
F/G
G
F/G
G
F/G
Gsus/B♭
3fr
Gsus/A
3fr
Gsus/A♭
3fr
C/G
C5

C/G
C
F/C
G/C
3fr
C
F/C
C/F
3fr
Gsus
3fr
G/C
3fr
C
F/C
G/C
3fr
C
F/C
C/F
3fr
Gsus
3fr
G/C
3fr
C
Might as well
jump.
Vocal ad lib.
F/C
G/C
3fr
C
F/C
C/F
3fr
Gsus
3fr
Repeat and Fade
Optional Ending
Go a-head and
jump.
Might as well
jump.
8vb

LA BAMBA

By RITCHIE VALENS

C
F
G7
C
F
G7
- ba; ar - ri - ba ar - ri - ba por tí se re
C
F
G7
por tí se re se re. Yo no soy mar - i -
C
F
G7
C
F
G7
ne - ro. Yo no soy mar - i - ne - ro, soy cap - i - tán;
C
F
G7
yo no soy mar - i - ne - ro, soy cap - i - tán.
To Coda

C
F
G7
C
F
G7
Bam - ba bam - ba, bam - ba bam -
C
F
G7
- ba, bam - ba, bam - ba,
C
F
G7
N.C.
D.S. al Coda
bam - ba bam. . . Pa - ra bai - lar la bam -
CODA
C
F
G7
Repeat and Fade
Optional Ending
C
Bam - ba, bam - ba!

LAYLA

Words and Music by ERIC CLAPTON
and JIM GORDON

Medium fast Rock
Fm
E♭
D♭
3fr
mf
Dm♭maj7
D♭maj7
1
2
Em
Bm7
2fr
What will you do___ when you get lone - ly
I tried___ to give___ you con - so - la - tion
So make___ the best___ of the sit - u - a - tion

Original key: E♭ minor. This edition has been transposed up one whole-step to be more playable.

Em
E♭
3fr
F
G
G7
and no - bod - y's wait - in' by your side?
when your old man, he let you down.
be - fore I fin - 'lly go in - sane.
Am7
Am/D
G
C
You been run - nin' and hid - in' much too long;
Like a fool, I fell in love with you;
Please don't say we'll nev - er find a way,
Am
D
G
C
you know it's just your fool - ish pride.
you turned my whole world up - side down.
and tell me all my love's in vain.
Lay -
Fm
D♭
E♭
3fr
Fm
la, you got me on my knees. Lay -

D♭maj7
E♭
Fm
D♭
la,
I'm beg - gin', dar - lin', please.
Lay - la,
dar - lin', won't you ease my wor - ried mind?
To Coda
1, 2
3
D.S. al Coda
Lay -
CODA
Slightly slower
E♭/G
A♭

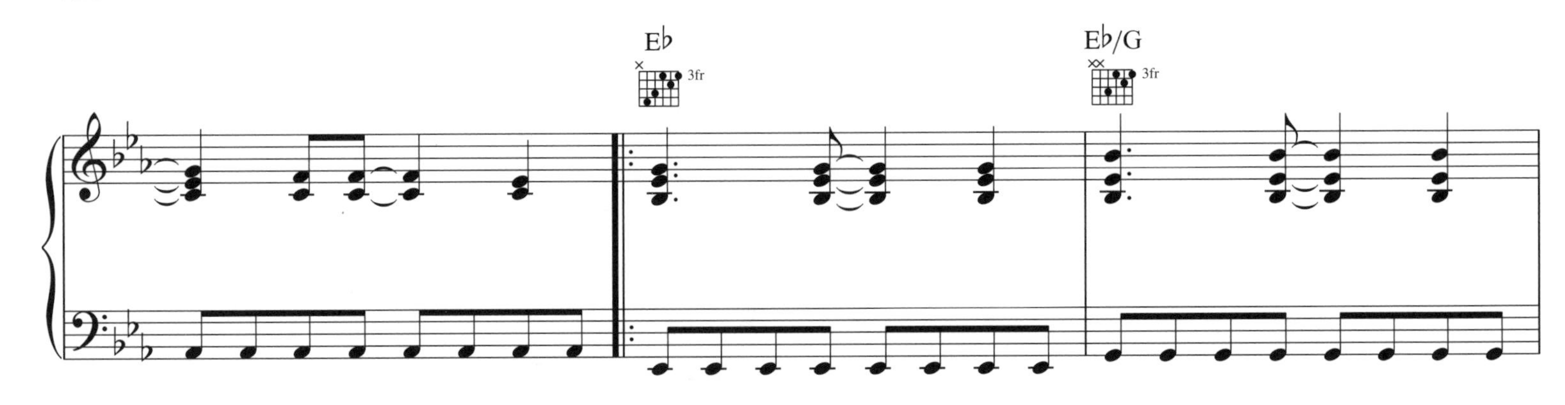
E♭
3fr
E♭/G
3fr

A♭
4fr
D♭9

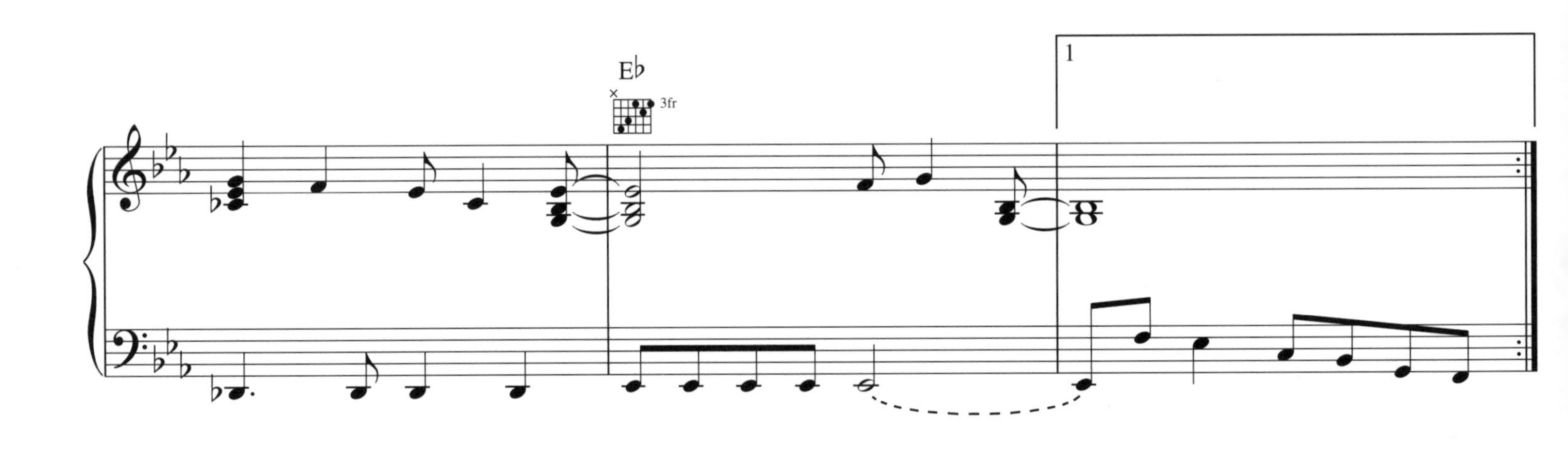
E♭
3fr
1

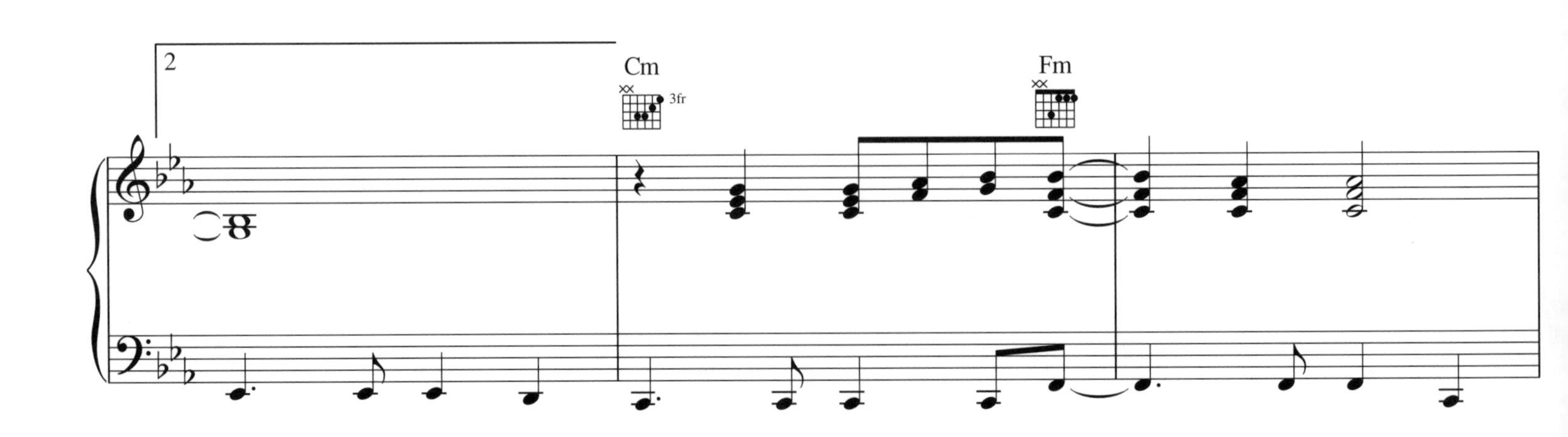
2
Cm
3fr
Fm

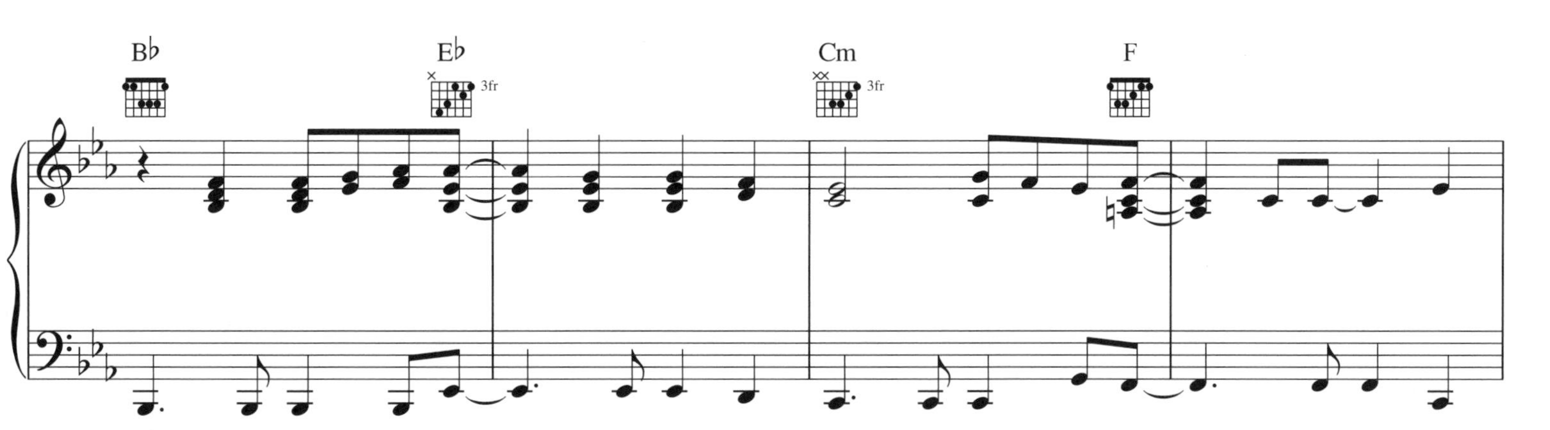
B♭
E♭
3fr
Cm
3fr
F

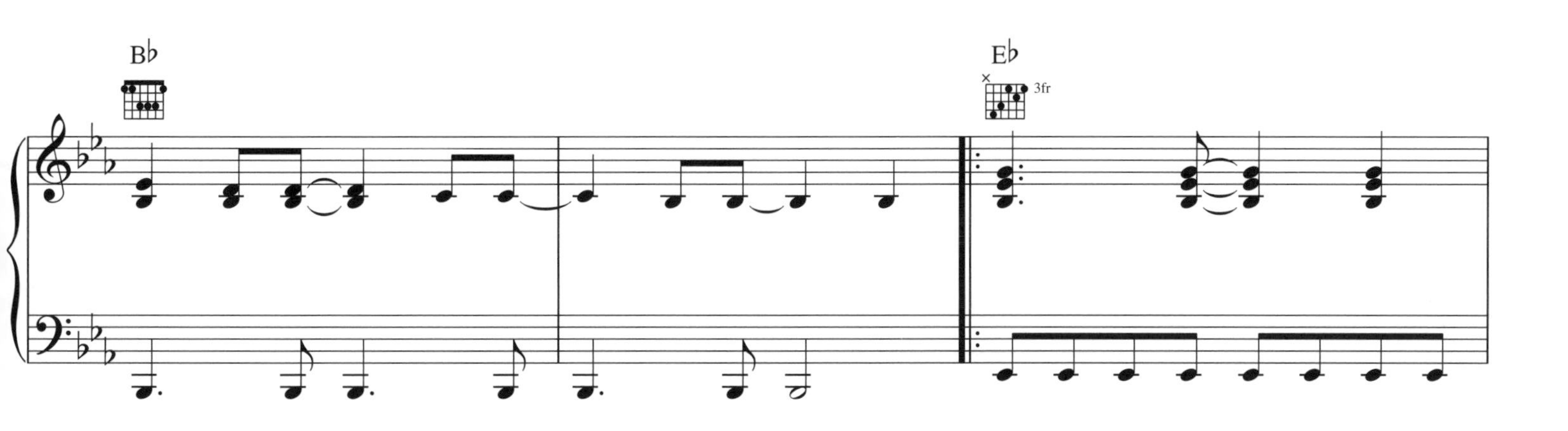
B♭
E♭
3fr

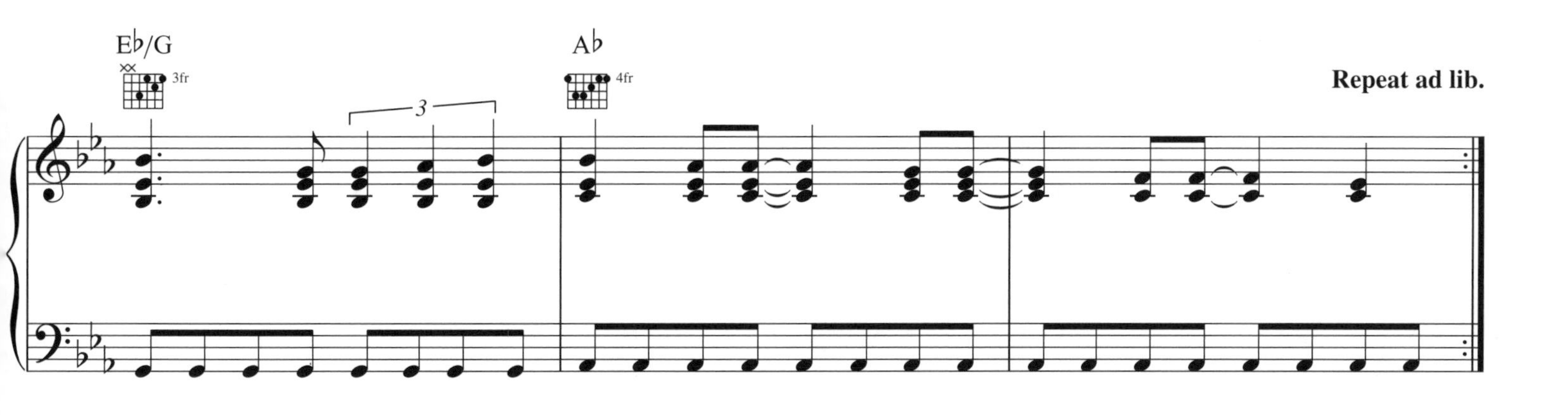
E♭/G
3fr
3
A♭
4fr
Repeat ad lib.

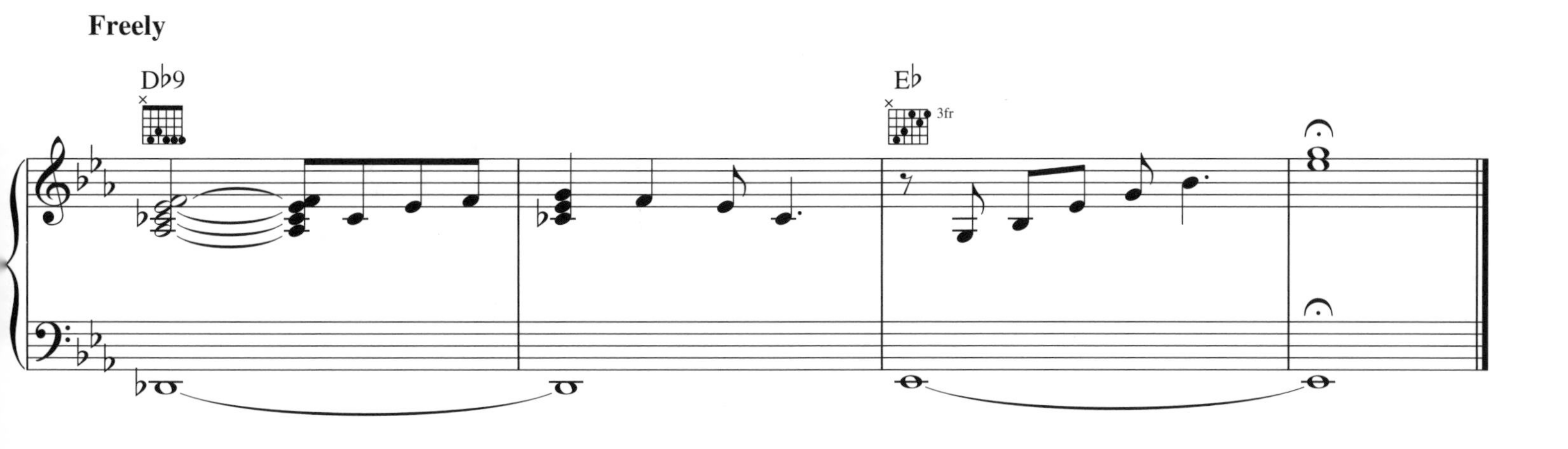
Freely
D♭9
E♭
3fr

LET IT BE

Words and Music by JOHN LENNON
and PAUL McCARTNEY

Slowly
C G Am F C/G G
mf
F C
C G
When I find my - self in times of trou - ble,
Instrumental
Am G F C G
Moth - er Mar - y comes to me speak - ing words of wis - dom; let it
F C/E Dm7 C G
be. And in my hour of dark - ness, she is

Am
G
F
C
G
stand-ing right in front _ of me ___ speak-ing words of wis - dom; let it
F
C/E
Dm7
C
G/B
Am
G
be. ___ Let it be, ___ let it be, ___ let it be, _
Instrumental ends
Let it be, ___ let it be, ___ let it be, _
F
C
G
let it be. ___ Whis-per words _ of wis - dom; let it be. _
let it be. ___ Whis-per words _ of wis - dom; let it be. _
F
C/E
Dm7
C
G
And when ___ the bro - ken - heart - ed peo - ple
And when ___ the night _ is cloud - y, there is

Am
G
F
C
G
liv - ing in the world a - gree there will be an an - swer, let it
still a light that shines on me. Shine un - til to - mor - row; let it
F
C/E
Dm7
C
G
be.
be.
For though they may be part - ed, there is
I wake up to the sound of mu - sic,
Am
G
F
C
G
still a chance that they will see there will be an an - swer; let it
Moth-er Mar - y comes to me speak-ing words of wis - dom; let it
F
C/E
Dm7
C
G/B
Am
G
be.
be.
Let it be, let it be, let it be,

F C G
let it be. There will be an an - swer; let it be.
F C/E Dm7 C G/B Am G
Let it be, let it be, let it be,
F C G
To Coda
let it be.
Whis - per words of wis - dom; let it be.
There will be an an - swer; let it be.
F C/E Dm7 C F Em Dm7 C B♭ F/A

G F C F C G F C
D.S. al Coda
CODA
F C/E Dm7 C G/B Am G
Let it be, let it be, let it be,
F C G
let it be. Whis-per words of wis - dom; let it be.
F C/E Dm7 C F Em Dm7 C B♭ F/A G F C

LIKE A ROLLING STONE

Words and Music by
BOB DYLAN

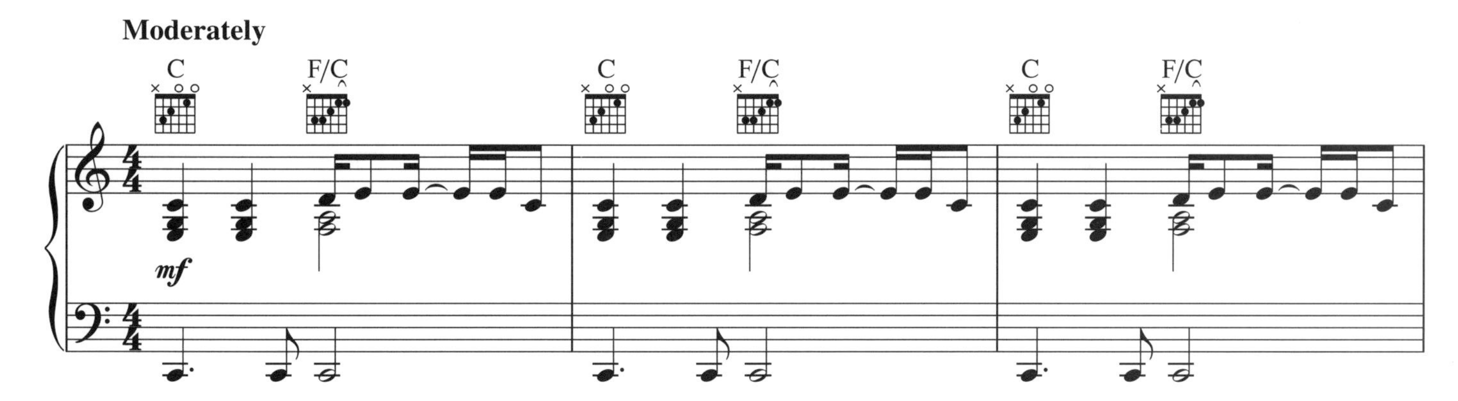
Moderately
C
F/C
C
F/C
C
F/C
mf

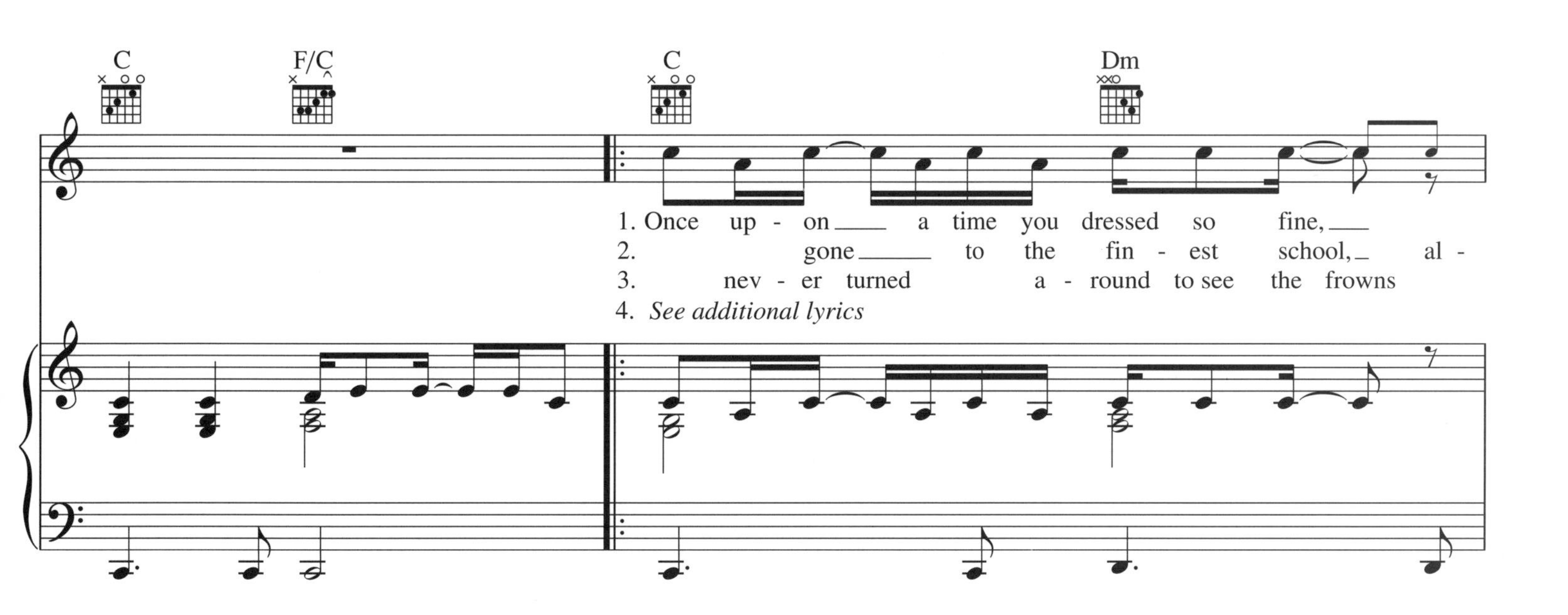
C
F/C
C
Dm
1. Once up - on a time you dressed so fine,
2. gone to the fin - est school, al -
3. nev - er turned a - round to see the frowns
4. See additional lyrics

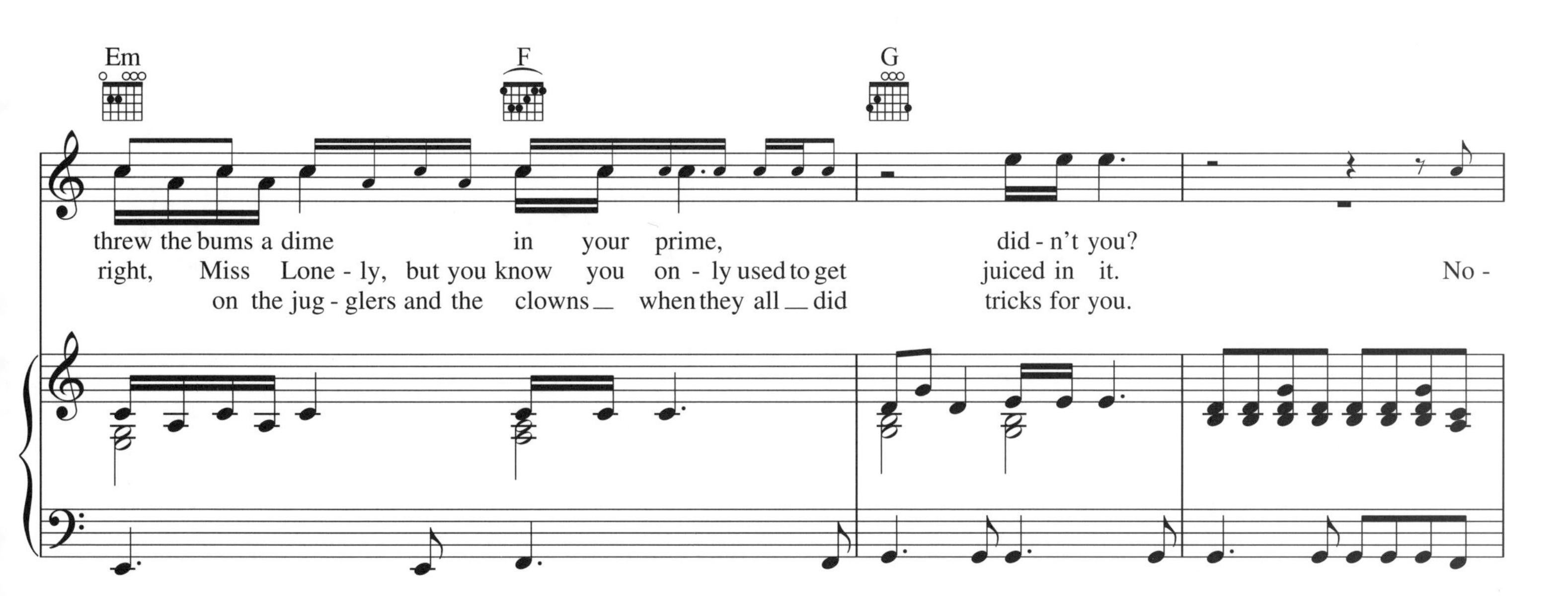
Em
F
G
threw the bums a dime in your prime, did - n't you?
right, Miss Lone - ly, but you know you on - ly used to get juiced in it. No -
on the jug - glers and the clowns when they all did tricks for you.

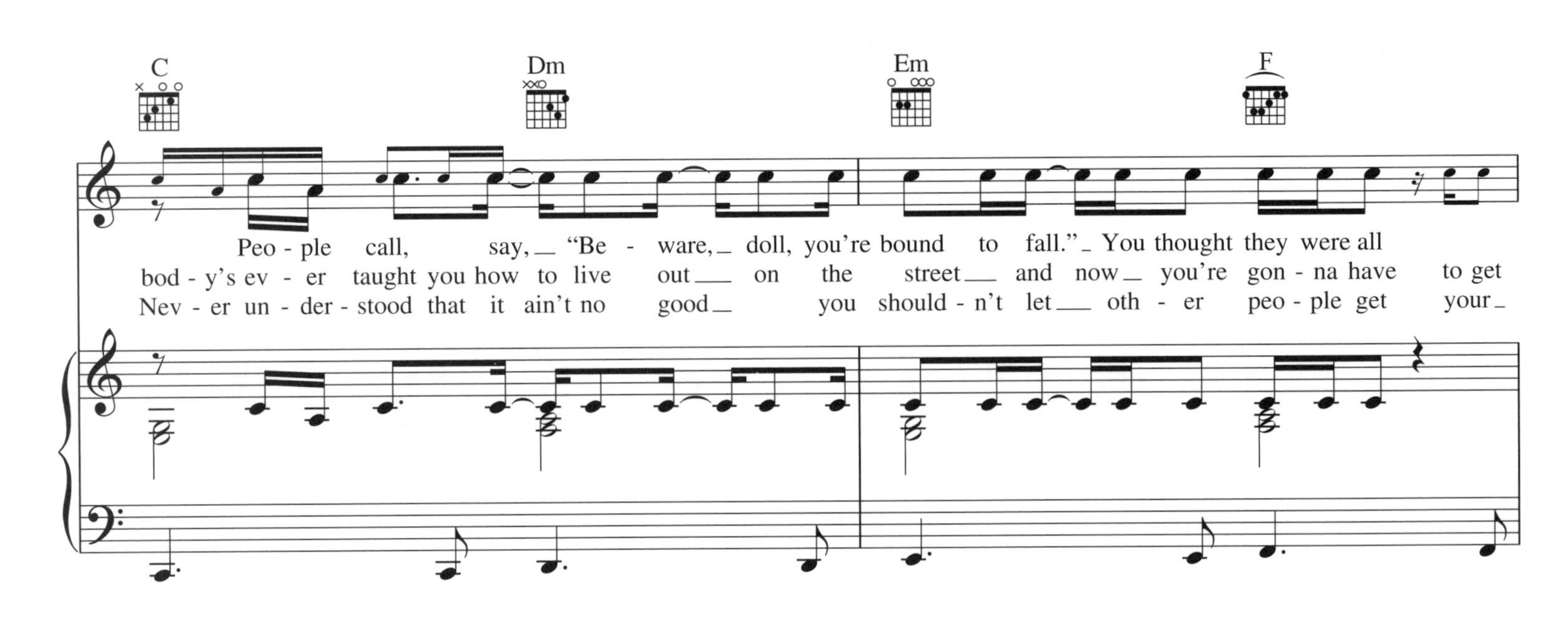
C
Dm
Em
F
Peo - ple call, say, "Be - ware, doll, you're bound to fall." You thought they were all
bod - y's ev - er taught you how to live out on the street and now you're gon - na have to get
Nev - er un - der - stood that it ain't no good you should - n't let oth - er peo - ple get your

G
F
a - kid - din' you. You used to
used to it. You say you
kicks for you. You used to ride on a chrome horse with your

G
F
G
laugh a - bout ev - 'ry - bod - y that was hang - in' out.
nev - er com - pro - mise with the mys - ter - y tramp, but now you re - al - ize
dip - lo - mat who car - ried on his shoul - der a Sia - mese cat.

F Em Dm C F Em
But now you don't talk so loud. Now you don't
he's not sell - ing an - y al - i - bis as you stare in - to the vac - uum
Ain't it hard when you dis - cov - er that he real - ly was - n't
Dm C Dm F
seem so proud a - bout hav - in' to be scroung - ing for your next
of his eyes and say, "Do you want to make a
where it's at af - ter he took from you ev - 'ry - thing he could
G C F G
Chorus
meal.
deal?"
steal.
How does it feel? How does it feel
C F G C F
to be with - out a home,
to be on your own,

G
C
F
1
like a com - plete un - known,
with no di - rec - tion home,
like a roll - ing stone?
Oh, you've
2, 3
a com - plete un - known,
like a roll - ing stone?
Oh, you

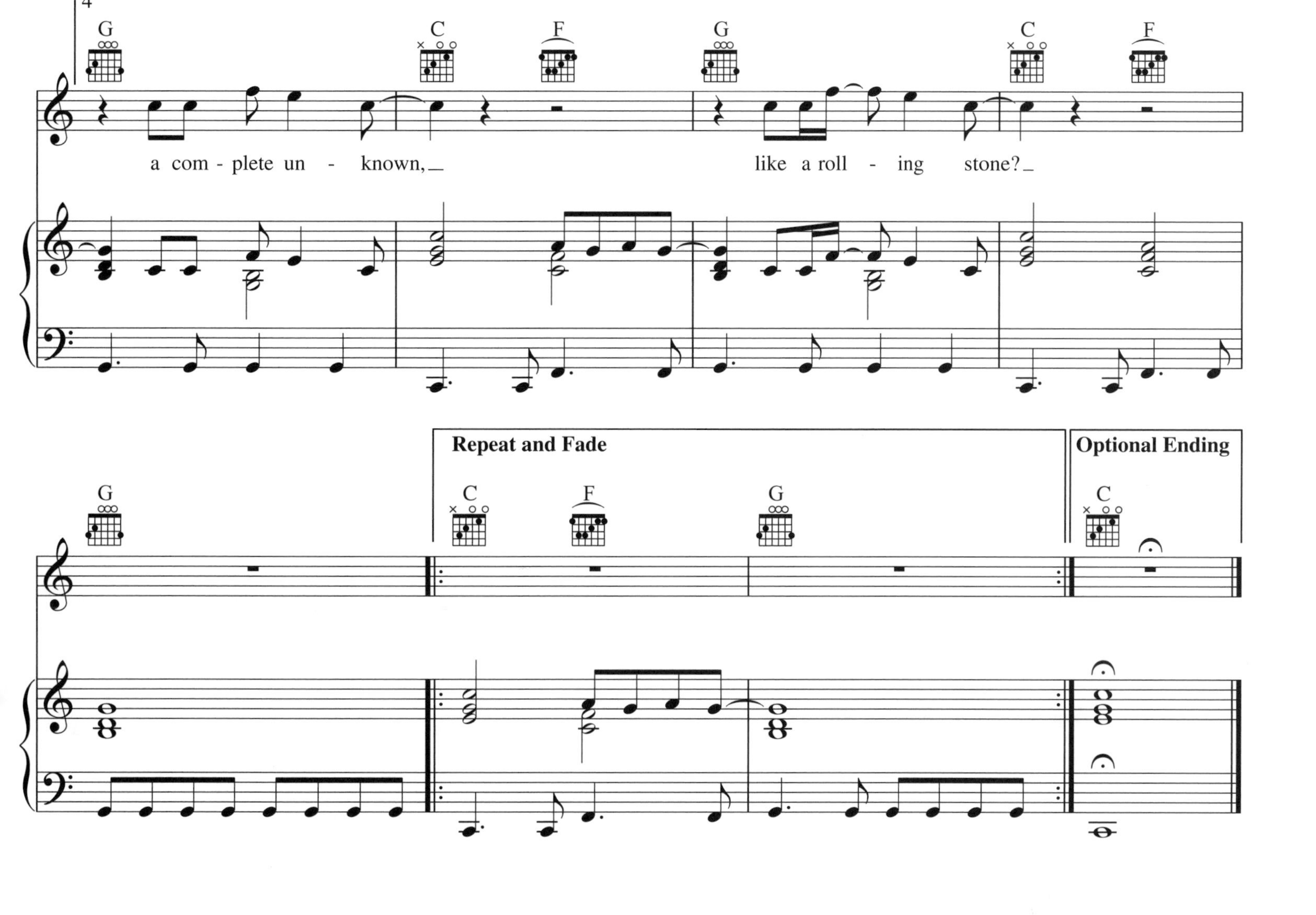

Additional Lyrics

4. Princess on the steeple and all the pretty people
   They're all drinkin', thinkin' that they got it made.
   Exchanging all precious gifts,
   But you better take your diamond ring,
   You'd better pawn it, babe.
   You used to be so amused
   At Napoleon in rags and the language that he used.
   Go to him now, he calls you, you can't refuse.
   When you got nothin', you got nothin' to lose.
   You're invisible now, you got no secrets to conceal.
   Chorus

LET'S STAY TOGETHER

Words and Music by AL GREEN,
WILLIE MITCHELL and AL JACKSON, JR.

Am7
Gm7
F
Em
'Cause you make me feel so brand
Let me be the one you come run - ning
You'd nev - er do that to
Dm9
3fr
Am7
Gm7
new, and now I want to
to. I'll nev - er
me, so be - ing a - round
F
Am7
Dm9
3fr
To Coda
1
spend my life with you. Let me say
be un - true.
you is all I see.
2
Gm9
3fr
Oh, ba - by, let's let's stay to -
3

Am7
Gm7
geth - er, loving you wheth - er, wheth-
B♭maj7
Am7
Dm
C
- er times are good or bad, hap - py or sad.
Gm9
3fr
A♭maj7
Gm9
3fr
A♭maj7
Gm7
Wheth - er times are

B♭maj7
Am7
Dm
C
D.S. al Coda
CODA
good or bad, hap - py or sad.
It's why I want us to:
Gm9
3fr
Am7
Let's let's stay to - geth - er,
3
Gm7
lov - ing you wheth - er, wheth - er times are
Optional Ending
Am7
Gm7
C
Repeat and Fade
F
good or bad, hap - py or sad.

LIGHT MY FIRE

Words and Music by
THE DOORS

Am7
F♯m7
If I was to say to you,
Try now we can on - ly lose, and our
Am7
F♯m7
girl, we could - n't get much higher.
love be - come a fu - neral pyre.
G
A
D
Come on, ba - by, light my fire.
G
A
D
B
G
D
Come on, ba - by, light my fire.
Try to set the night on

E
1, 2
3
fire.
The
You
cresc.
f
Am7
F♯m7
Am7
know that it would be un - true,
you know that I would be a liar,
F♯m7
Am7
F♯m7
if I was to say to you,
Am7
F♯m7
G
A
girl, we could-n't get much higher.
Come on, ba - by, light my fire.

D
G
A
D
Come on, ba - by, light my fire.
F
C
D
Play 3 times
F
C
Try to set the night on fire.
Try to set the night on
ff
D5
5 fr
G
D
fire.
F
B♭
E♭
3 fr
A♭
4 fr
A
3

LONDON CALLING

Words and Music by JOE STRUMMER,
MICK JONES, PAUL SIMONON
and TOPPER HEADON

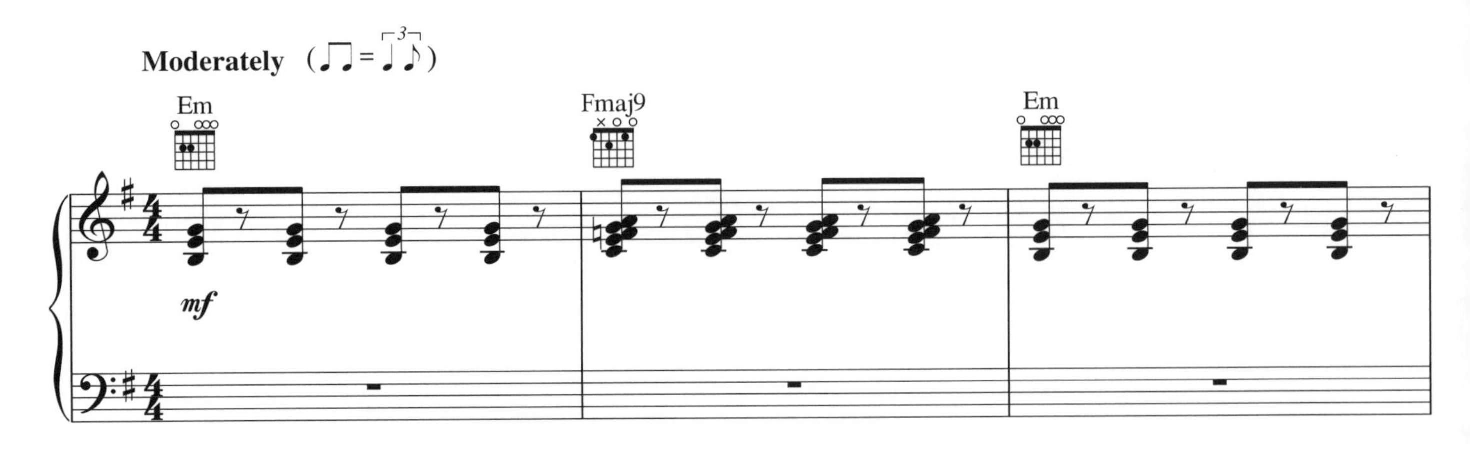

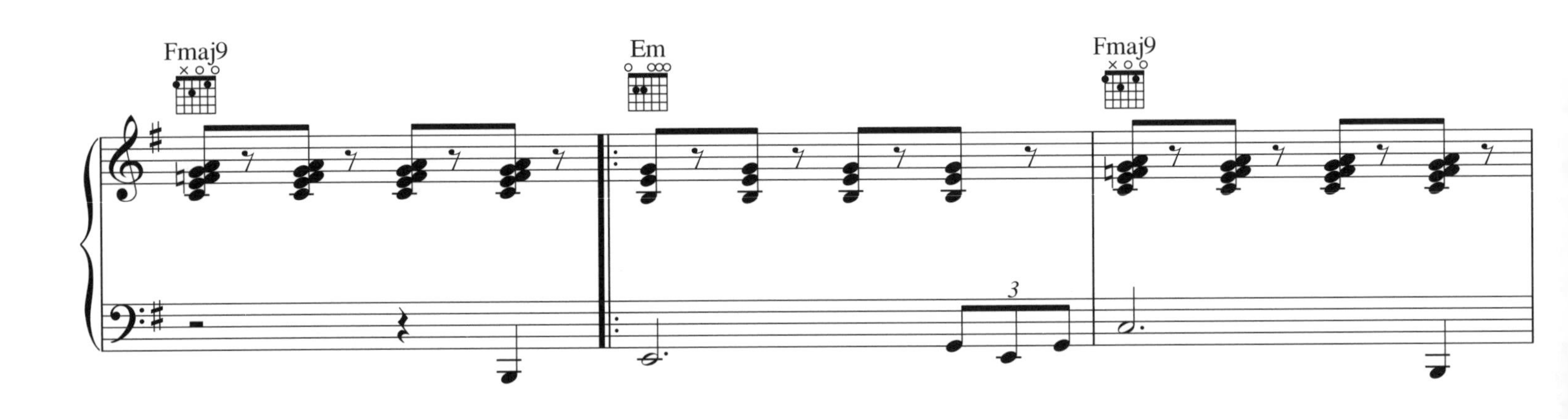

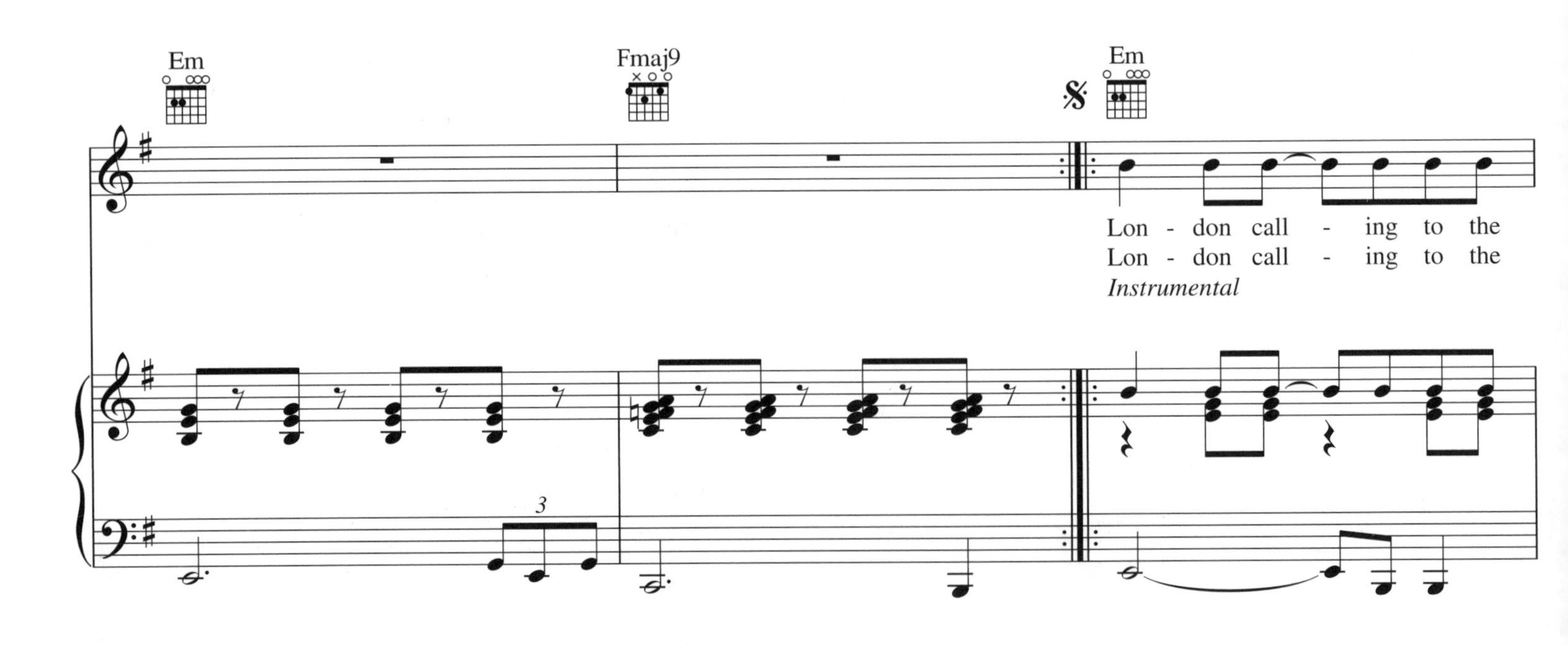

Fmaj9
Em/G
G
far - a - way towns. Now war is de - clared and bat - tle come down.
im - i - ta - tion zone. For - get it, broth - er. You can go it a - lone.
Em
Fmaj9
Em/G
3
Lon - don call - ing to the un - der - world. Come out of the cup - board, you
Lon - don call - ing to the zom - bies of death. Quit hold - ing out and
G
Em
Fmaj9
boys and girls. Lon - don call - ing. Now, don't look to us.
draw an - oth - er breath. Lon - don call - ing. And I don't want to shout. But
Em/G
G
Em
3
Pho - ny Beat - le - ma - ni - a has bit - ten the dust. Lon - don call - ing. See, we
while we were talk - ing, I saw you nod - ding out. Lon - don call - ing. See, we

Fmaj9
Em/G
G
ain't got no swing, ex - cept for the ring of the trun-cheon thing. The
ain't got no highs, ex - cept for that one with the yel - low - y eyes. The
End instrumental
Em
G
D
Em
ice age is com - ing. The sun's zoom - ing in. Melt - down ex - pect - ed. The
ice age is com - ing. The sun's zoom - ing in. En - gines stop run - ning. The
G
D
Em
G
D
wheat is grow - ing thin. En - gines stop run - ning. But I have no fear, 'cause
wheat is grow - ing thin. A nu - cle - ar er - ror. But I have no fear, 'cause
Em
To Coda
D
1
Lon - don is drown - ing and I live by the riv - er.
Lon - don is drown - ing and I I live by the riv - er.

2
D.S. al Coda
live by the riv - er.
CODA
D
I
I live by the riv - er.
Em
Fmaj9
Em
Fmaj9
Em
Fmaj9
Em
Fmaj9
Em
Now get this.
Lon - don call - ing. Yes,

Fmaj9
Em
Fmaj9
I was there, too. And you know what they said? Well, some of it was true!
Em
Fmaj9
Em
London calling at the top of the dial. And after all this, won't you
Fmaj9
Em
Fmaj9
give me a smile? London calling.
Em
Fmaj9
Em
I never felt so much alike...

MORE THAN A FEELING

Words and Music by
TOM SCHOLZ

D
Csus2
G/B
G
lost my - self in a fa - mil - iar song. I
I still re - call as I wan - der on, as
D
Cadd2
G/B
closed my eyes and I slipped a - way.
clear as the sun in the sum - mer sky.
Am
G
D
G
C
Em
D
G
C

Em
D
G
C
Em
D
It's more than a feel - ing
when I
(More than a feel - ing.)
G
C
Em
D
hear that old song they used to play,
and
(More than a feel - ing.)
G
C
Em
D
I be - gin dream - ing
till I
(More than a feel - ing.)
G
C
To Coda
E♭
6fr.
Em7
see Mar - i - anne walk a - way.
I see my Mar -

1.
A
G
D/F♯
Em7
i - anne walk - in' a - way.
D
Csus2
G/B
G
D
Csus2
G/B
G
2. Bm
Bm/A
G
D/F♯
Asus4
A
Ah.
D
G
D/F♯
A
D
G

D/F♯
A
D
G
Bm
A/C♯
D
Bm
Em7
A
G
D/F♯
Em7
D
Csus2
G/B
G
D
Csus2
G/B
G
D
Csus2
G/B
G
D
When I'm tired___ and think - ing cold,
I hide in my mu - sic, for -

Csus2 G/B G D Csus2 G/B G
get the day and dream of a girl I used to know. I
D Csus2 G/B Csus2 D
closed my eyes and she slipped a - way.
Csus2 G/B Csus2 D Csus2 G/B G D
She slipped a - way.
Csus2 G/B Csus2 D Csus2 G/B

Am
G
D
D.S. al Coda
Coda
Em
D
G
C
way.
Em
D
G
C
Em
D
C
Repeat and fade
G
C
Em
D
G
C
Em
D

LOUIE, LOUIE

Words and Music by
RICHARD BERRY

A
D
Em
D
A
D
Em
D
A
D
Em
D
1, 2
A
D
Em
D
3
A
D
Em
D
D.S. al Coda
CODA
A
D
Em
D
A
D
Em
D
A
D
Em
D
A

MAGGIE MAY

Words and Music by ROD STEWART
and MARTIN QUITTENTON

Moderately bright
D
Em
G
mf
D
A
G
Wake up, Mag - gie, I think I got some - thing to
D
A
say to you:
It's late Sep - tem - ber and I
G
D
real - ly should be back at school.
I

G D G A
know I keep you a - mused, but I feel I'm be - ing used. Oh,
Em F♯m Em7
Mag - gie, I could - n't have tried an - y - more. You
Em A Em A
lured me a - way from home, just to save you from be - ing a - lone. You
(2., 3.) See additional lyrics
Em A D
stole my heart and that's what real - ly hurts. The

A
G
D
morn - ing sun, when it's in your face, real - ly shows your age. But
that don't wor - ry me none; in my eyes you're ev - 'ry - thing. I
laughed at all of your jokes, my love you did - n't need to coax. Oh,
Em
F♯m
After last verse, skip to Coda
D.S. for extra verses
Mag - gie, I could - n't have tried an - y - more.
2. You
3. You

Additional Lyrics

2. You lured me away from home, just to save you from being alone.
   You stole my soul, that's a pain I can do without.
   All I needed was a friend to lend a guiding hand.
   But you turned into a lover, and, Mother, what a lover! You wore me out.
   All you did was wreck my bed and in the morning kick me in the head.
   Oh, Maggie, I couldn't have tried any more.

3. You lured me away from home 'cause you didn't want to be alone.
   You stole my heart, I couldn't leave you if I tried.
   I suppose I could collect my books and get back to school,
   Or steal my Daddy's cue and make a living out of playing pool,
   Or find myself a rock and roll band that needs a helpin' hand.
   Oh, Maggie, I wish I'd never seen your face. *(To Coda)*

MY GENERATION

Words and Music by
PETER TOWNSHEND

F
Eb
Bb
Hope I die be-fore I get old.
This is my gen-er-
[Talk-in' 'bout my gen-er-a-tion]
a-tion,
This is my gen-er-a-tion, ba-by.
Why don't you all fade a-way?
[Talk-in' 'bout my gen-er-a-tion]
Don't try and dig what we all say.
I'm
[Talk-in' 'bout my gen-er-a-tion]

F
Eb
F
Bb
Eb
not tryin' to cause a big sen - sa - tion. I'm just
[Talk - in' 'bout my gen - er - a - tion]
F
Eb
F
Bb
Eb
talk - in' 'bout my gen - er - a - tion.
[Talk - in' 'bout my gen - er - a - tion]
This is my gen - er -
F
Eb
F
Eb
a - tion,
This is my gen - er - a - tion, ba - by.
1.
2.
NC
F
Eb6
F

NO WOMAN NO CRY

Words and Music by
VINCENT FORD

C
G/B
Am
F
said I re - mem - ber
(D.S.) Said I re - mem - ber
when we used to sit
in the gov - ern - ment yard in Trench - town.
1. O - ba, O - b - serv - ing the hyp - o - crites as they would
2.,3. And then Geor - gie would make a fi - re - light as it was
min - gle with the good peo - ple we meet,
log wood burn - in' through the night.

C
G/B
Am
F
good friends we had, oh good friends we've lost
Then we would cook corn - meal por - ridge
a - long the way.
of which I'll share with you.
In this bright fu - ture you can't for - get your past,
My feet is my on - ly car - riage,
so, dry your tears I say. And
so, I've got to push on through, but while I'm gone I mean...
To Coda

C G/B Am F G

Ev - 'ry - thing's gon - na be al - right. Ev - 'ry - thing's gon - na be al - right.

C G/B 1 Am F G

Ev - 'ry - thing's gon - na be al - right. Ev - 'ry - thing's gon - na be al - right.

2 Am F C G/B

Ev - 'ry - thing's gon - na be al - right so, wom - an, no cry.

3

Am F C F C

No, no wom - an, no wom - an, no cry.

C
G
C
G/B
Oh, my lit - tle sis - ter,
Am
F
C
F
C
don't shed no tears.
No wom - an, no cry.
G
C
G/B
Am
F
Guitar solo - ad lib.
C
F
C
4
G
5
G
D.S. al Coda
Solo ends

CODA
C
G/B
Am
F
No wom - an, no cry.
C
F
C
G
No wom - an, no cry.
C
G/B
Am
F
Oh, my lit - tle dar - lin', I say don't shed no tears.
C
F
C
G
No wom - an, no cry.
Yeah.

C
G/B
Am
F
Lit - tle dar - lin', don't shed no tears.
Vocal tacet 3rd time
C
F
C
G
Play 3 times
No wom - an, no cry.
C
G/B
Am
F
C
F
C

MY GIRL

Words and Music by WILLIAM "SMOKEY" ROBINSON
and RONALD WHITE

F
C
Dm7
F
G
C
Dm7
I guess you'll say, what can make me
F
G
Cmaj9
feel this way?
My girl, (my girl,) (my girl,) talk - in' 'bout
Dm7
C/D
G7
Dm7
G
C
To Coda
my girl. (My girl.) I've got so much
F
C
F
hon - ey, the bees en - vy me. I've got a

C
F
C
sweet - er song
than the birds
in the trees.
F
D.S. al Coda
Well,
C/D
G7
Dm7
G
C
CODA
(My girl.)
Ooh,
hoo.
F
C
F
Dm7
(Hey, hey, hey.)
(Hey, hey, hey.)

G
Em
A
Ooh, hoo, yeah. I don't
D
G
need no mon - ey, for - tune,
D
G
D
or fame. I've got all the rich-es, ba - by,
G
D
G
one man can claim. Well,

D
Em7
G
A
D
Em7
I guess you'll say, what can make me
G
A
Dmaj9
4 fr
feel this way? My girl, (my girl,)
Em7
(my girl,) talk - in' 'bout my girl.
A
G
Dmaj7/F♯
Em
Dmaj9
4 fr
(My girl.) (Talk - in' 'bout my girl,
I've got sun - shine on a

Em7
whoa whoa.)
cloud - y day with my girl; I've
A G Dmaj7/F# Em Dmaj9
4 fr
(Talk - in' 'bout my girl, my girl,
e - ven got the month of May with my girl.
Em7
my girl, whoa whoa.)
Talk - in' 'bout, talk - in' 'bout, talk-in' 'bout my girl.
3
Repeat and Fade
A G Dmaj7/F# Em
(Talk - in' 'bout
Optional Ending
A G Dmaj7/F# Em Dmaj9
4 fr

OH, PRETTY WOMAN

Words and Music by ROY ORBISON
and BILL DEES

D
E7
wom - an
I don't be - lieve you, you're not the
wom - an
that you look love - ly as can
truth
No one could look as good as
be
Are you lone - ly just like
N.C.
you.
me?
Mer - cy.
1
E7
2
E7
Pret - ty

Dm
G7
Pret - ty wom - an stop a - while,
C
Am
Dm
Pret - ty wom - an talk a - while,
Pret - ty wom - an
G7
C
give your smile to me.
Dm
G7
C
Pret - ty wom - an yeah, yeah, yeah,
Pret - ty wom - an

Am
Dm
look my way,
Pret - ty wom - an
G7
C
A7
say you'll stay with me.
'Cause I
F♯m
Dm
E7
need you
I'll treat you right.
A
F♯m
Dm
Come with me ba - by.
Be mine to -

E7
night.
A
F♯m
Pret - ty wom - an don't walk on by, Pret - ty
A
F♯m
wom - an don't make me cry, Pret - ty
D
E7
wom - an don't walk a - way.

Hey,
O. K.
If that's the way it must be
O. K.
I guess I'll go on home, it's late
There'll be to - mor - row night but wait!
N.C.
What do I see?

E7
Is she walk - ing back to
me?
Yeah, she's
walk - ing back to me!
A
Oh, Pret - ty wom - an.

PIANO MAN

Words and Music by
BILLY JOEL

F C/E D7 G

reg - u - lar crowd shuf - fles in. There's an
gets me my drinks for free, and he's
nev - er had time for a wife, and he's
man - ag - er gives me a smile 'cause he

C Em/B Am C/G

old man sit - ting next to me mak - in'
quick with a joke or to light up your smoke, but there's
talk - in' with Da - vy, who's still in the Na - vy and
knows that it's me they've been com - in' to see to for -

F G11 C F/C

love to his ton - ic and gin.
some - place that he'd rath - er be.
prob - a - bly will be for life.
get a - bout life for a - while.

Cmaj7 G11 C Em/B

He says, "Son, can you play me a
He says, "Bill, I be - lieve this is
And the wait - ress is prac - tic - ing
And the pia - no sounds like a

mf

Am
C/G
F
C/E
mem - o - ry?
I'm not real - ly sure how it
kill - ing me,"
as a smile ran a - way from his
pol - i - tics
as the bus - 'ness - men slow - ly get
car - ni - val,
and the mi - cro - phone smells like a
D7
G
C
Em/B
goes,
but it's sad and it's sweet and I
face.
"Well, I'm sure that I could be a
stoned.
Yes, they're shar - ing a drink they call
beer,
and they sit at the bar and put
Am
C/G
F
G11
3fr
knew it com - plete when I wore a young - er man's
mov - ie star if I could get out of this
lone - li - ness, but it's bet - ter than drink - in' a -
bread in my jar and say, "Man, what are you do - in'
C
Am
Am/G
clothes."
Da da da de de
place."
Da da da de de
lone.
Instrumental
here?"
Da da da de de
mp

D7/F♯
F
Am
Am/G
da, da da de de
da, da da de de
da, da da de de
D7/F♯
D7
G
G/F
C/E
da da da.
da da da.
Instrumental ends
da, da da.
G7/D
C
Em/B
Am
C/G
Sing us a song, you're the pia - no man.
f
F
C/E
D7
G
C
Sing us a song to - night. Well, we're all in the

Em/B
Am
C/G
F
G11
3fr
mood for a mel - o - dy, and you've got us feel - in' al -
C
F/C
Cmaj7
1-3
G11
4
G11
right.
Now
Now
It's a
C
Em/B
Am
C/G
F
mf
G11
C
F/C
Cmaj7
F/C
C
G7/C
C
F/C
Cmaj7
F
C/E
Dm7
C

PAPA WAS A ROLLIN' STONE

Words and Music by NORMAN WHITFIELD
and BARRETT STRONG

Moderately fast
Am7
mf

1
2
It was the third of Sep - tem - ber.
nev - er got a chance to see

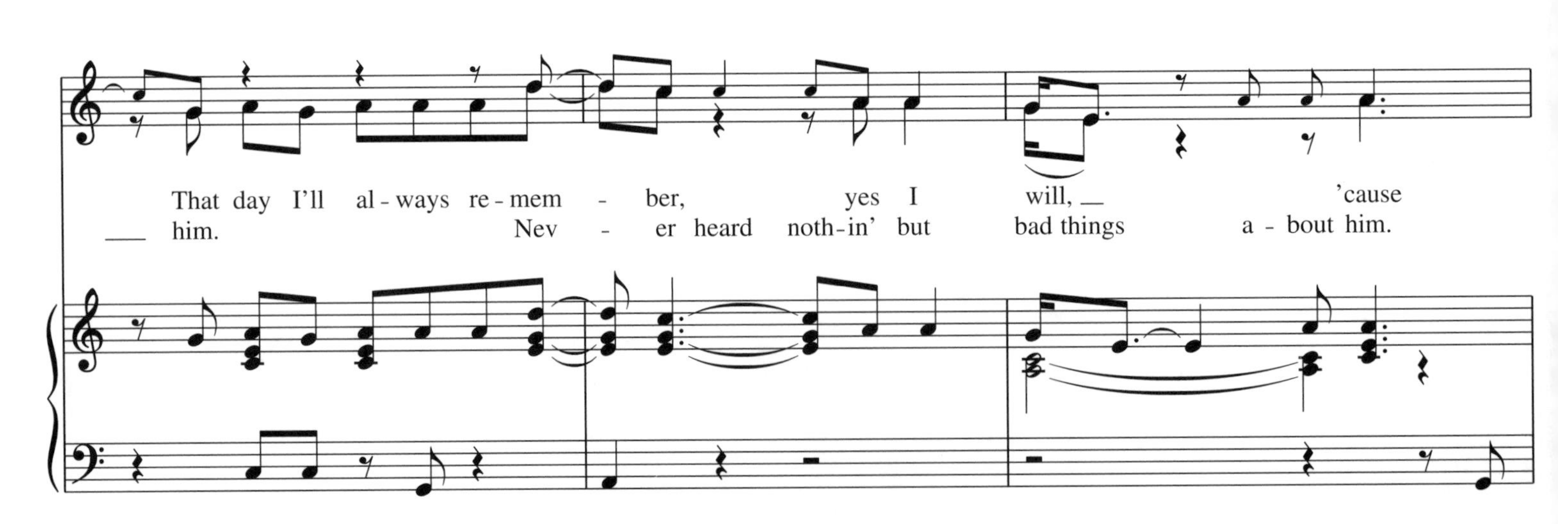
That day I'll al - ways re - mem - ber, yes I will, 'cause
him. Nev - er heard noth - in' but bad things a - bout him.

1
that was the day
that my dad - dy died.
Ma - ma, I'm de - pend - ing on you to tell me the truth.
2
I
Spoken: Mama just hung her head and said, "Son,
Pa - pa was a roll - in' stone."
Wher - ev - er he laid his hat
was his home.
And when he died,
all he left us was a -

1,3
2,4
lone.
Hey Ma - ma,
is it true what they say, that Pa - pa nev - er worked a day in
Heard some talk a - bout Pa - pa do - in' some store-front preach-in'.
I heard Pa - pa call him - self a Jack - of - all - trades. Tell
Folks say Pa - pa nev - er was much on think - in'.
3
3
his life?
And Ma - ma,
Talk - in' 'bout sav - in' souls and all the time preach - ing,
me, is that what sent Pa - pa to an ear - ly grave?
Spent most of his time chas - in' wom - en and drink - ing.
bad talk goin' a - round town say that Pa - pa had three out - side chil - dren
heal - ing and then steal-ing in the name of the Lord.
folks say Pa - pa would beg, bor-row, steal to
Ma - ma, I'm de-pend - ing on you to tell me the

1,3
2
D.S.
and an - oth - er wife.
And that ain't right.
Spoken:
Mama just hung her head and said,
pay his bills.
Hey, Ma - ma,
truth.
4
Mama looked up with a tear in her eye and said,
"Pa - pa was a roll - in' stone."
Wher - ev - er he laid his hat was his home.
And when he died, all
he left us was a - lone.
Repeat and Fade

PROUD MARY

Words and Music by
J.C. FOGERTY

A
wor - ry'n' 'bout the way things might have been.
till I hitched a ride on a riv - er - boat queen.
Peo - ple on the riv - er are hap - py to give.
Big wheel, keep on turn -
Bm
D
- in', proud Ma - ry keep on burn - in'. Roll - in', roll-
1
To Coda
- in', roll - in' on the riv - er.
2
C
A
- in' on the riv - er.

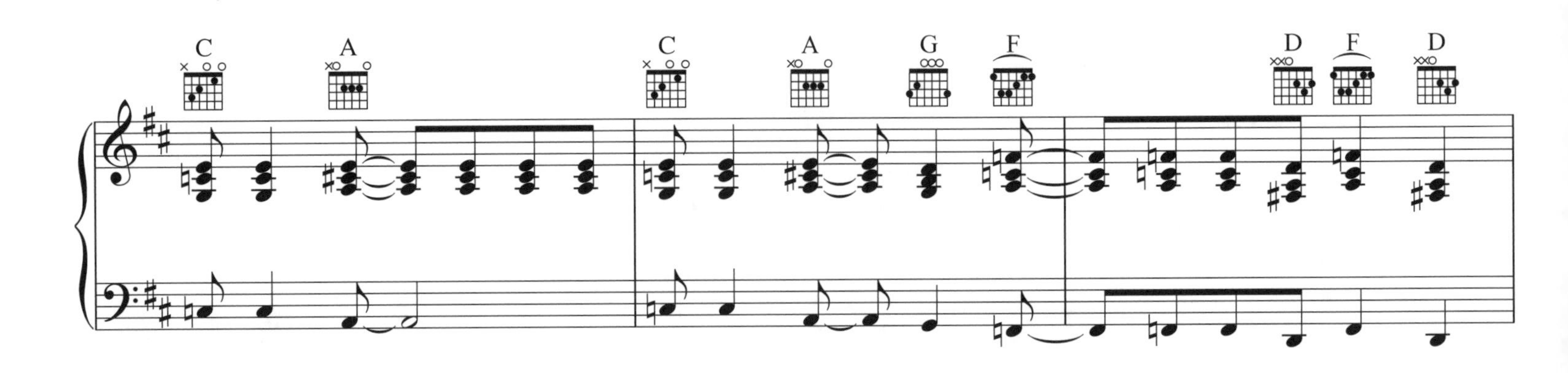
C
A
C
A
G
F
D
F
D

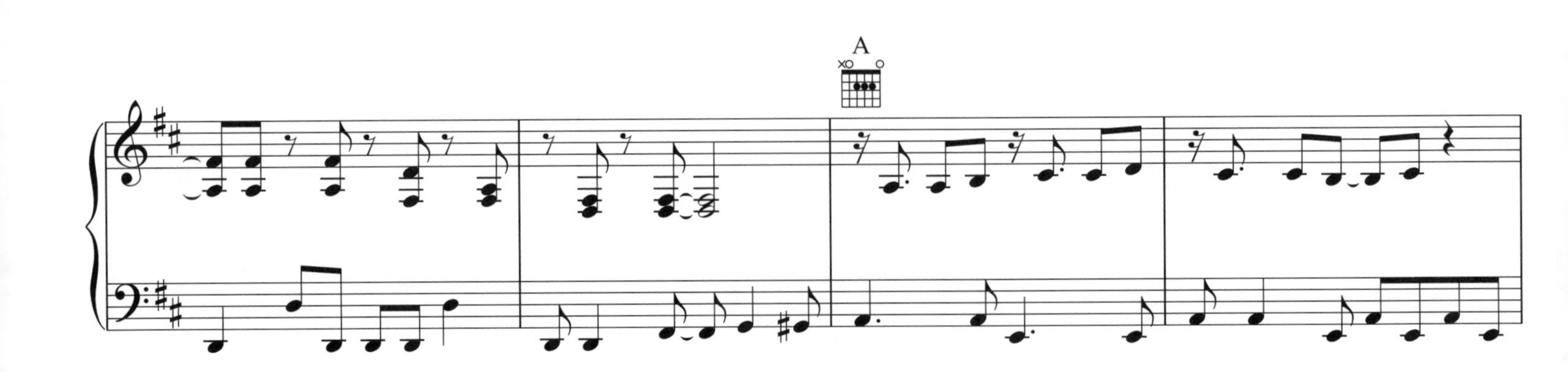
A

Bm
D
Roll - in', roll - in', roll - in' on the riv - er.
C
A
G
F
D.S. al Coda

CODA
- in' on the riv - er.
Roll - in',
roll - in',
roll - in' on the riv - er.
Roll-
Repeat and Fade
Optional Ending
C
A
C
A
C
A
G
F
D
F
D

PURPLE HAZE

Words and Music by
JIMI HENDRIX

F
no chord
C
'Scuse me __ while I kiss the sky.
3
F
Ab
Bb
F
4
Pur - ple haze ____ all a - round, Don't know if I'm com - in'
Ab
Bb
F
up or down, Am I hap - py or
Ab
Bb
F
no chord
in mi - se - ry? __ What - ev - er it is, __ that girl put a

C
spell on me.
(Spoken: Help me, help me ah oh no no.)
F
Ab
Bb
F
Pur - ple haze was in my eyes,
Don't know if it's
Ab
Bb
F
Ab
Bb
day or night.
You got me blow - in'
blowin' my mind, is it
F
no chord
C7#5
F7#9
to- mor - row or just the end of time?

RESPECT

Words and Music by
OTIS REDDING
Solid 4 Beat
mf
G
F
f
What you want baba - by I got.
I ain't gon-na do you wrong while you gone.
What you need You know I got it.
I ain't gon-na do you wrong 'Cause I don't wan - na.

G
F
C7
All I'm ask-in' is for a lit-tle re-pect, when you come home. Ba-
F
C7
F
-by, when you come home,___ Re-spect.
G
F
G
I'm out___ to give you all my mon-ey, But all I'm ask-in'
Ooh,___ your kiss-es, sweeter than hon-ey, But guess___ what,___
F
G
in re-turn, hon-ey, Is to give me
so here's my mon-ey, All I want you to do for me

F
C
my pro-per res - pect when you get home. Yeah,
is give me some here when you get home. Yeah,
F
C7
F
ba - by, when you get home.
ba - by, when you get home.
C7
F
C7
R - E - S - P - E - C - T, find out what it means to me, R - E - S - P - E - C - T,
F
C7
F
Repeat and fade out
take out T - C - P, a lit-tle re - pect.

SEXUAL HEALING

Words and Music by MARVIN GAYE, ODELL BROWN and DAVID RITZ

A♭
E♭
B♭
Cm
Ooo
Ba
Ba
Gm7
A♭
E♭
by, I'm hot just like an ov-
by, I got sick this morn-
B♭
Cm
Gm7
A♭
E♭
en; I need some lov - in'.
in', A sea was storm - in' in-
B♭
Cm
Gm7
side of me.
Ba
Ba

Ab
Eb
Bb
Cm
by,
I can't hold it much longer;
by,
I think I'm cap - siz - in',
Gm7
Ab
Eb
It's get - tin' strong - er and strong - er.
The waves are ris - in' and ris - in'. And
Bb
Cm
Gm7
Ab
Eb
When I get that feel - in' I want sex - u - al
When I get that feel - in' I want sex - u - al
Bb
Cm
Gm7
heal - ing, sex - u - al heal - ing.
heal - ing, sex - u - al heal - ing.

Ab
Eb
Bb
Cm
Oh ba - by, makes me
(It's good for me) makes me
Gm7
Ab
Eb
feel so fine,
feel so fine,
(It's sumpcherous)
Bb
Cm
Gm7
Ab
Eb
Helps to re - lieve my mind.
Helps to re - lieve my mind. (And
Bb
Cm
Gm7
Sex - u - al heal - ing
it's good for us) Sex - u - al heal - ing

A♭
E♭
B♭
Cm
ba - by is good for me. Sex - u - al
ba - by is good for me. Sex - u - al
Gm7
Fm7
Gm7
A♭maj7
A♭/B♭
To Coda
heal - ing is some - thing that's good for me.
heal - ing is some - thing that's good for me.
E♭
G7
When - ev - er blue tear - drops are fall - ing
A♭maj7
And my e - mo - tion - al sta -

Fm7 Gm7 A♭maj7 A♭/B♭ E♭
bil - i - ty is leav - ing me There is some -
G7
- thing I can do: I can
A♭maj7 Fm7 Gm7
get on the tel - e - phone and call you up, ba -
A♭maj7 A♭/B♭ E♭
- by. Say Hon - ey, I know you'll be there

G7
Abmaj7
to re - lieve me 'cause the love you
Fm7
Gm7
Abmaj7
Ab/Bb
Eb
give to me will be.
G7
If you don't know the thing you're deal - ing,
Abmaj7
I can tell you dar - lin', that it's

Fm7
Gm7
A♭maj7
A♭/B♭
B♭
Cm
sex - u - al heal - ing.
Get up, get up,
Gm7
A♭
E♭
get up, get up, Let's make love to - night!
B♭
Cm
Gm7
A♭
E♭
Wake up, wake up, wake up, wake up, 'cause you do it right!
D.S. al Coda
CODA
E♭
And it's good for me,

G7
A♭maj7
And it's so good to me, my ba -
Fm7
Gm7
A♭maj7
A♭/B♭
by. Oh Oh,
E♭
G7
come take con - trol
Just grab a hold
A♭maj7
of my bod - y and mind;
Soon we'll be

Fm7
Gm7
A♭maj7
A♭/B♭
E♭
mak - in' it hon - ey, Oh, we'll be do - in', fine. You're my med -
G7
- e - cine, O - pen up and let me in.
A♭maj7
Fm7
Gm7
Dar - lin', you're so pret - ty, I can't wait for you to
A♭maj7
A♭/B♭
B♭
Cm
Gm7
op - er - ate.
(heavy breathing)

A♭
E♭
B♭
Cm
Let's make love to - night!
Wake up, wake up,
Gm7
A♭
E♭
wake up, wake up, 'cause you do it right!
B♭
Cm
Gm7
A♭
E♭
B♭
Cm
Gm7
A♭
E♭
Repeat and Fade

ROCK AROUND THE CLOCK

Words and Music by MAX C. FREEDMAN
and JIMMY DeKNIGHT

F7
Bb9
clock strikes one.
yell for more.
sev - enth heav'n.
so will you.
clock a - gain.
We're gon - na rock a - round the clock to night, we're gon - na
F
G7
rock, rock, rock, 'til broad day - light. We're gon - na rock, gon - na rock a - round
Gm7
C7#5
C9sus
1-4
F
the clock to - night.
2. When the
3. When the
4. When it's
5. When the
5
F

ROXANNE

Written and Composed by
G.M. SUMNER

Gsus4
Cm
Fsus4
Gsus4
put on the red light Rox - anne you don't have to put on the red light
G7sus4
To Coda
Cm
Bb
Eb
F
F
Gm
Rox - anne Rox - anne Rox - anne
(put on the red light) (put on the red light)
F/C
Bb
F/C
Eb
F
Gsus4
Rox - anne Rox - anne Oh
(put on the red light) (put on the red light) (put on the red light)
D.%. al Coda
CODA
Gm
Gm/F
Gm
Gm/F
Bb
I
(-anne)
(put on the red light)
Repeat to fade
Eb
F
F
Gm
F/C
Bb
Rox - anne Rox - anne Rox - anne
(put on the red light) (put on the red light)

SHE LOVES YOU

Words and Music by JOHN LENNON
and PAUL McCARTNEY

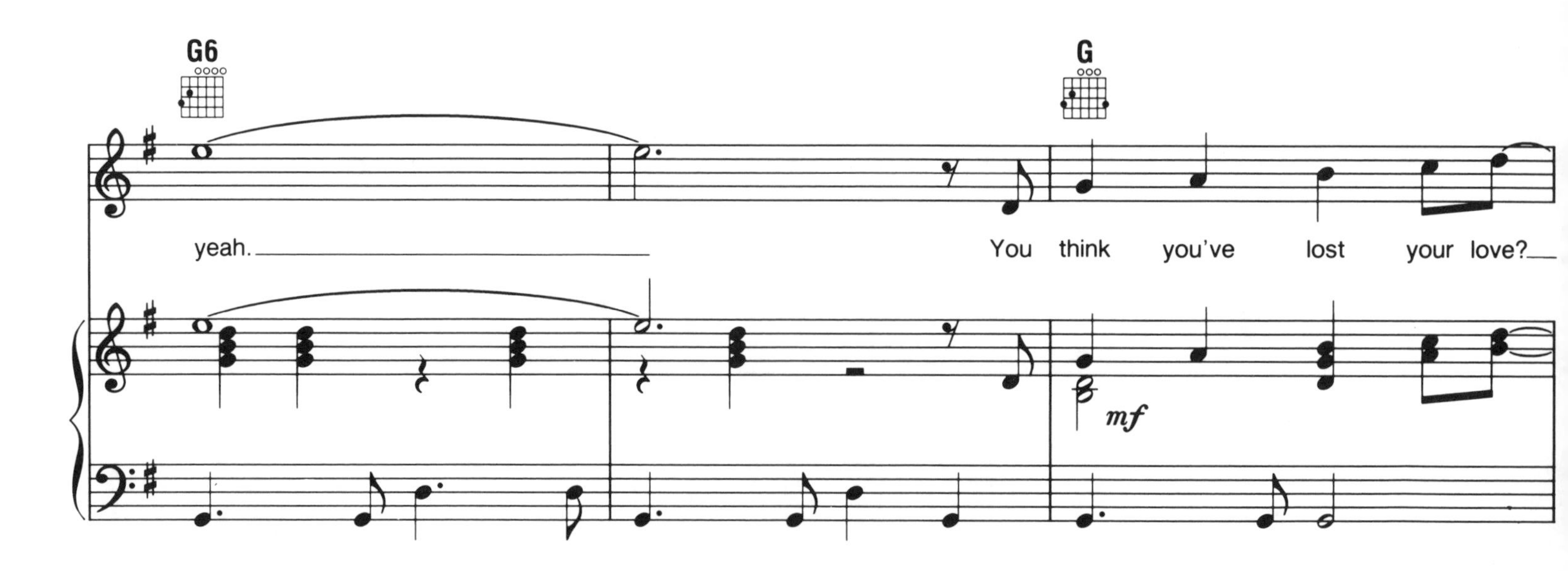

Em
Bm
D
Well, I saw her yes - ter - day.
It's
G
Em
Bm
you she's think - ing of
And she told me what to
D
G6
say:
She says she loves you and you know that can't be
Em
Cm6
bad.
Yes, she loves you and you

D
know you should be glad. She
G Em Bm
said you hurt her so, She al - most lost her
know it's up to you, I think it's on - ly
D G Em
mind. But now she says she knows You're
fair. Pride can hurt you too A -
Bm D G6
not the hurt - ing kind. She says she
pol - o - gize to her. Be-cause she
loves you and you

Em
Cm6
know that can't be bad.
Yes, she loves you and you
D
Em
know you should be glad. oo!
She loves you, yeah,
A7
yeah, yeah,
She loves you, yeah,
yeah, yeah. And with a
Cm6
D+
D7
1
G
love like that you know you should be glad.
You

G
Em
Cm6
With a love like that you
D+
D7
G
Em
Cm6
know you should be glad.
With a love like that you
D+
D7
G
Em
know you should be glad. Yeah, yeah, yeah,
Yeah,
rit.
a tempo
C
G6
yeah, yeah,
Yeah, yeah, yeah, yeah!

SMELLS LIKE TEEN SPIRIT

Words and Music by KURT COBAIN,
CHRIS NOVOSELIC and DAVID GROHL

F5/A♭ F5/D♭ F5 F5/B♭ F5/A♭ F5/D♭

self - as - sured. Oh, no, I know a dirt - y word.
has al - ways been and al - ways will un - til the end.
it was hard to find. Oh, well, what - ev - er, nev - er mind.

F5 F5/B♭ F5/A♭ F5/D♭ F5 F5/B♭

Hel - lo, hel - lo, hel - lo. How low? Hel - lo, hel - lo,

F5/A♭ F5/D♭ F5 F5/B♭ F5/A♭ F5/D♭

hel - lo. How low? Hel - lo, hel - lo, hel - lo. How low?

F5 F5/B♭ F5/A♭ F5/D♭ F5 B♭5

Hel - lo, hel - lo, hel - lo. With the lights out it's less dan -

Ab5 Db5 F5 Bb5 Ab5 Db5
-g'rous. Here we are now; en-ter-tain us. I feel stu-
F5 Bb5 Ab5 Db5 F5 Bb5
-pid and con-ta-gious. Here we are now; en-ter-tain
Ab5 Db5 F5 Bb5 Ab5 Db5
us. A mu-lat-to, an al-bi-no, a mos-qui-
To Coda
F5 Bb5 Ab5 Db5 F5 E5 F5 Gb5
N.C.
-to, my li-bi-do. Yeah! Oy.

F5 E5 F5 B♭5 A♭5 4fr F5 E5 F5 G♭5 F5 E5 F5 B♭5 A5 5fr A♭5 4fr
N.C.
Oy.
1
F5 F5/B♭ 3fr F5/A♭ 3fr F5/D♭ 3fr F5 F5/B♭ 3fr F5/A♭ 3fr F5/D♭ 3fr
2
F5 B♭5 A♭5 4fr D♭5 4fr F5 B♭5 A♭5 4fr D♭5 4fr
F5 B♭5 A♭5 4fr D♭5 4fr F5 B♭5 A♭5 4fr D♭5 4fr

F5
Bb5
Ab5
Db5
F5
Bb5
Ab5
Db5
Play 3 times
F5
F5/Bb
F5/Ab
F5/Db
D.S. al Coda
F5
F5/Bb
F5/Ab
F5/Db
CODA
F5
Bb5
- to, my li - bi -
Ab5
Db5
F5
Bb5
Ab5
Db5
Play 4 times
F5
- do. A de - ni - al, a de - ni - al. A de - ni - al.

SOMEBODY TO LOVE

Words and Music by
DARBY SLICK

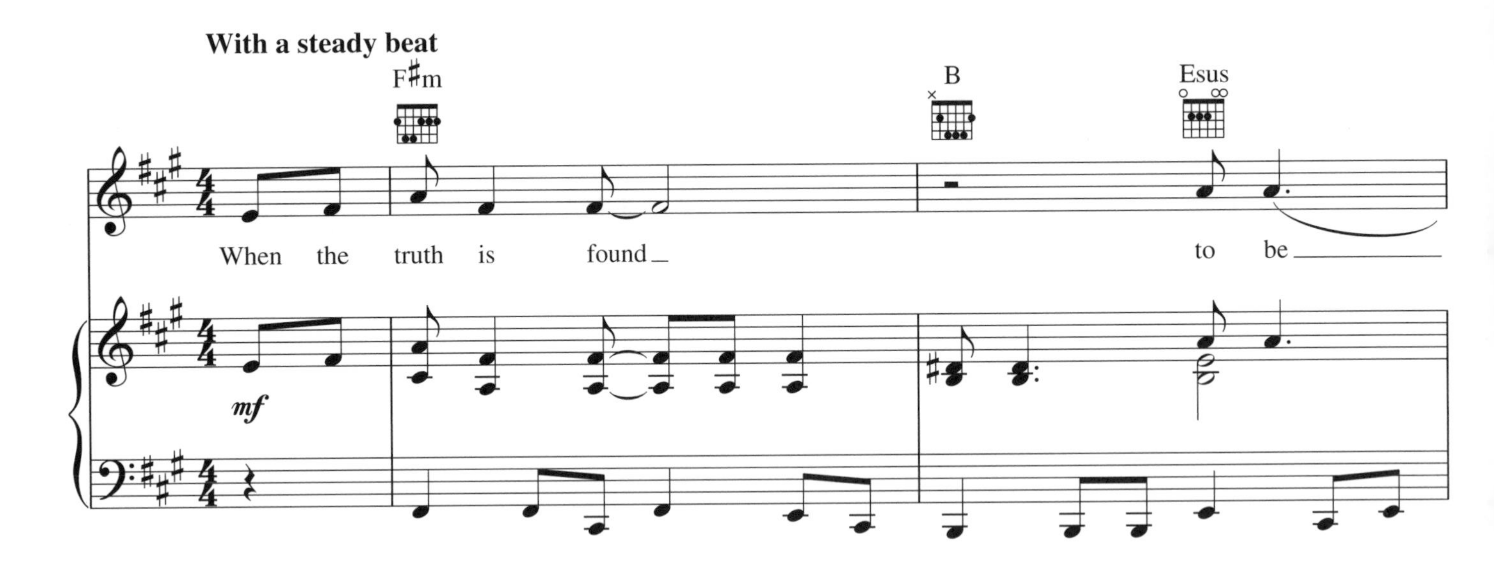

A E F♯m B A E
want some - bod - y to love? Don't you need some - bod - y to love?
F♯m B A E
Would - n't you love some - bod - y to love?
F♯m B A B F♯m B
You bet - ter find some - bod - y to love.
F♯m E

F♯m
When the gar - den's flow - ers,
B
Esus
F♯m
ba - by, are
dead, yes, and
B
E
F♯m
your mind, your mind is so full of red,
B
A
E
F♯m
B
don't you want some - bod - y to love? Don't you

A
E
F♯m
B
need some - bod - y to love? Would - n't you
A
E
F♯m
B
A
B
love some - bod - y to love? You bet - ter find some - bod - y to love.
F♯m
Your eyes, I say your eyes may
look like his. Yeah, but

F#m B F#m
in your head, ba - by, I'm a - fraid you don't know where it is.
B A E F#m B
Don't you want some - bod - y to love? Don't you
A E F#m B A E
need some - bod - y to love? Would - n't you love some - bod - y to love?
F#m B A B F#m E
You bet - ter find some - bod - y to love.

B
A
F♯m
Tears are run - ning,
B
F♯m
B
E
they're all run - ning down your breast,
and
F♯m
B
E
F♯m
your friends, ba - by,
they treat you
like a guest.

A
E
B
Don't you want some - bod - y to love?
Don't you
need some - bod - y to love?
Would - n't you love some - bod - y to love?
F♯m
You bet - ter find some - bod - y to love.
Bsus2
7fr

STAND BY ME

Words and Music by BEN E. KING,
JERRY LEIBER and MIKE STOLLER

F
see, oh I won't be a - fraid
sea, I won't cry, I won't cry
Dm C Dm
no I won't be a - fraid
no I won't shed a tear
just as
B♭ C F
long as you stand, stand by me.
So
F
dar - ling, dar - ling, stand by me

Dm
C
Dm
B♭
stand by me oh stand
C
F
1
2
stand by me stand by me.
If the
Darling,
F
Dm
C
Dm
stand by me
stand by me oh
B♭
C
F
Repeat and Fade
stand
stand by me
stand by me.
When-ev-er I'm in trou-ble won't you

SPACE ODDITY

Words and Music by
DAVID BOWIE

C
Em
Com-men-cing count down: En-gines on.
Six, Five, Four, Three,
Am
Am7
D7
C9♯11
Check ig-ni-tion and may God's love be with you.
Two, One, Lift off!
Space craft lift off music
cresc.
C
E7
F
This is ground control to Ma-jor Tom; You've real-ly made the grade! And the
This is Ma-jor Tom to ground con-trol; I'm step-ping thro' the door, And I'm
Fm
C
F
Fm
C
pa-pers want to know whose shirts you wear. Now it's time to leave the cap-sule if you dare
float-ing in a most pe-cu-li-ar way. And the stars look ve-ry dif-fer-ent to day

F
Fmaj7
Em7
2nd (For) here am I sit-ting in a tin can
Here am I float-ing round my tin can
mf
Fmaj7
Em7
Bbmaj7
Am9
G9
2nd Fret
Far a-bove the world Plan-et Earth is blue and there's nothing I can
Far a-bove the moon Plan-et Earth is blue and there's nothing I can
F
C
G
A
do.
do.
f
Em7
A9
C9
D9/E
6th Fret
E9
Last time repeat ad lib. for Fade ending
ad lib. Solo
Fine
Though I'm past one hun-dred thous-and miles

E7
F
Fm
C
I'm feel-ing ve-ry still
And I think my space-ship knows which way to go
F
Fm
C
F
Tell my wife I love her ve-ry much. "She knows"
G
E7b9
Am
Am7
"Ground con-trol to Ma-jor Tom: Your cir-cuit's dead. There's some-thing wrong. Can you
D7
C
G
hear me Ma-jor Tom? Can you hear me Ma-jor Tom? Can you hear me Ma-jor Tom? Can you"
D.S. al Fine

START ME UP

Words and Music by MICK JAGGER
and KEITH RICHARDS

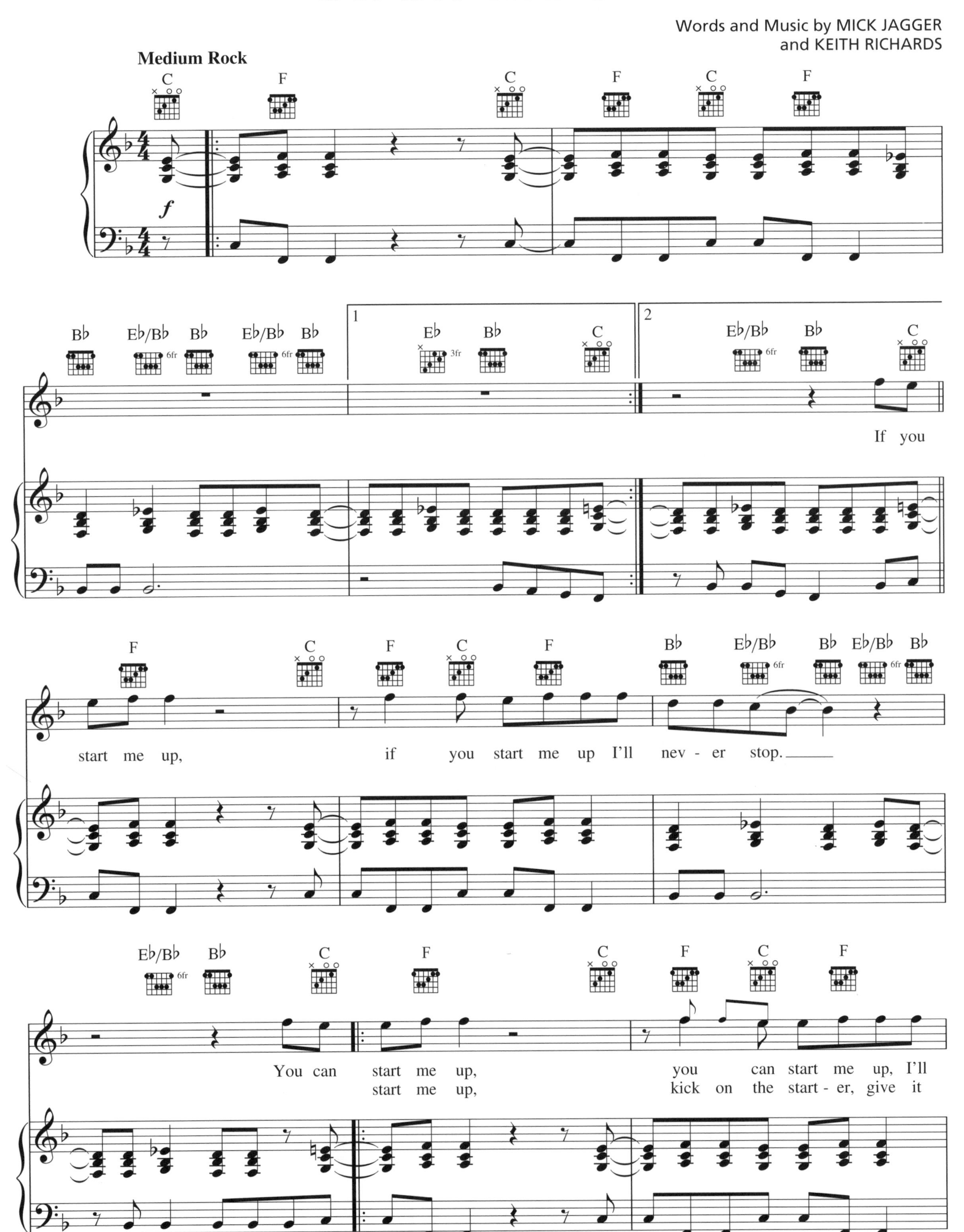

B♭ E♭/B♭ B♭ E♭/B♭ B♭ E♭ B♭ C F C
6fr 6fr 3fr
nev - er stop.
all you've got.
(You got, you got.)
I've been run - ning hot,
I can't com - pete
Start me up,
F C F B♭ E♭/B♭ B♭ E♭ B♭ E♭/B♭ B♭ C
6fr 3fr 6fr
you got me just a - bout to blow my top.
with the ri - ders in the oth - er heats.
ah you've got to, you've got to, nev - er nev - er, nev - er stop.
You can
You
F C F C F B♭ E♭/B♭ B♭ E♭ B♭
6fr 3fr
start me up, you can start me up, I nev - er stop, nev - er stop,
rough it up, if you like it you can slide it up, slide it up,
Start it up, ah start it up,
C F
nev - er stop, nev - er stop. You make a grown man cry,
slide it up, slide it up. Don't make a grown man cry,
nev - er, nev - er, nev - er. You make a grown man cry,

C F C F
you make a grown man cry, you make a grown man
don't make a grown man cry, don't make a grown man
you make a grown man cry, you make a grown man
C F C F C F C
cry. Spread out the oil, the gas - o - line,
cry. My eyes di - late, my lips go green,
cry. Ride like the wind at dou - ble speed,
To Coda
Cm7 Bb C F C
3fr
I walk smooth ride in a mean, mean ma - chine.
my hands are grea - sy, she's a mean, mean ma - chine.
I'll take you plac - es that you've nev - er, nev - er seen.
F C F Bb Eb/Bb Bb Eb/Bb Bb
6fr 6fr
Start it up.
Start it up.
1
Eb Bb C
3fr
You can

2
E♭/B♭
B♭
C
6fr
D.S. al Coda
CODA
C
F
C
F
C
F
B♭
E♭/B♭
B♭
E♭/B♭
B♭
E♭/B♭
B♭
C
If you
F
C
F
C
F
start it up, love the day when we will
Tough me up,
You, you, you make a grown man
Repeat and Fade
B♭
E♭/B♭
B♭
E♭/B♭
B♭
E♭/B♭
B♭
C
nev - er stop, nev - er stop,
nev - er stop, nev - er stop,
cry.
nev - er, nev - er, nev - er stop.

STAYIN' ALIVE
from the Motion Picture SATURDAY NIGHT FEVER

Words and Music by BARRY GIBB,
MAURICE GIBB and ROBIN GIBB

Bb7
all right.— It's O K.— And you may look— the oth - er way.—
all right.— It's O K.— I'll live to see— an - oth - er day.—
We can try— to un - der - stand. the New York Times'— ef - fect— on man..
Fm7
Wheth-er you're a broth-er or wheth - er you're a moth-er, you're stay - in' a - live,— stay - in' a - live.—
Feel the cit - y break-in' and ev - 'ry-bod - y shak - in', and we're stay-in' a - live,— stay - in' a - live.—

Ah, ha, ha, ha, stay-in' a-live, stay-in' a-live. Ah, ha, ha, ha,
Fm
Eb/F
Fm
stay-in' a-live.
Cm7
To Coda
1. Fm7
Well now, I
2. Fm7
Bb7
Life go-in' no-where.

Fm7
Some-bod - y help me.
Some-bod - y help me, yeah.
Bb7
Life go - in' no where.
Some-bod - y help me, yeah.
Fm7
D.S. al Coda (lyric 1)
Stay-in' a - live.
Well, you can tell
CODA
Fm7
Bb7
Life go - in' no - where.

Some - bod - y help me.
Some - bod - y help me, yeah.
Fm7
Bb7
Life go - in' no - where.
Some - bod - y help me, yeah.
Fm7
I'm stay - in' a - live.
Repeat and Fade

STRAWBERRY FIELDS FOREVER

Words and Music by JOHN LENNON
and PAUL McCARTNEY

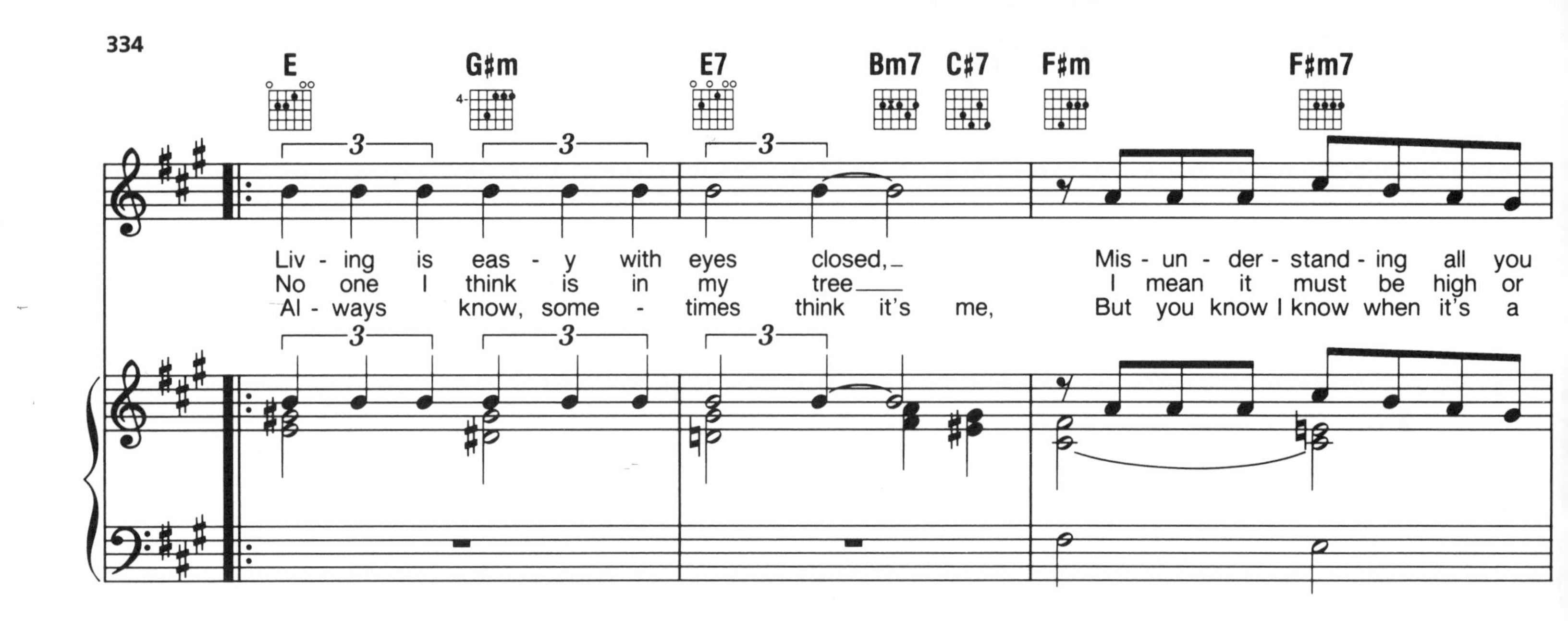
E
G#m
E7
Bm7
C#7
F#m
F#m7
Liv - ing is eas - y with eyes closed, Mis - un - der - stand - ing all you
No one I think is in my tree I mean it must be high or
Al - ways know, some - times think it's me, But you know I know when it's a

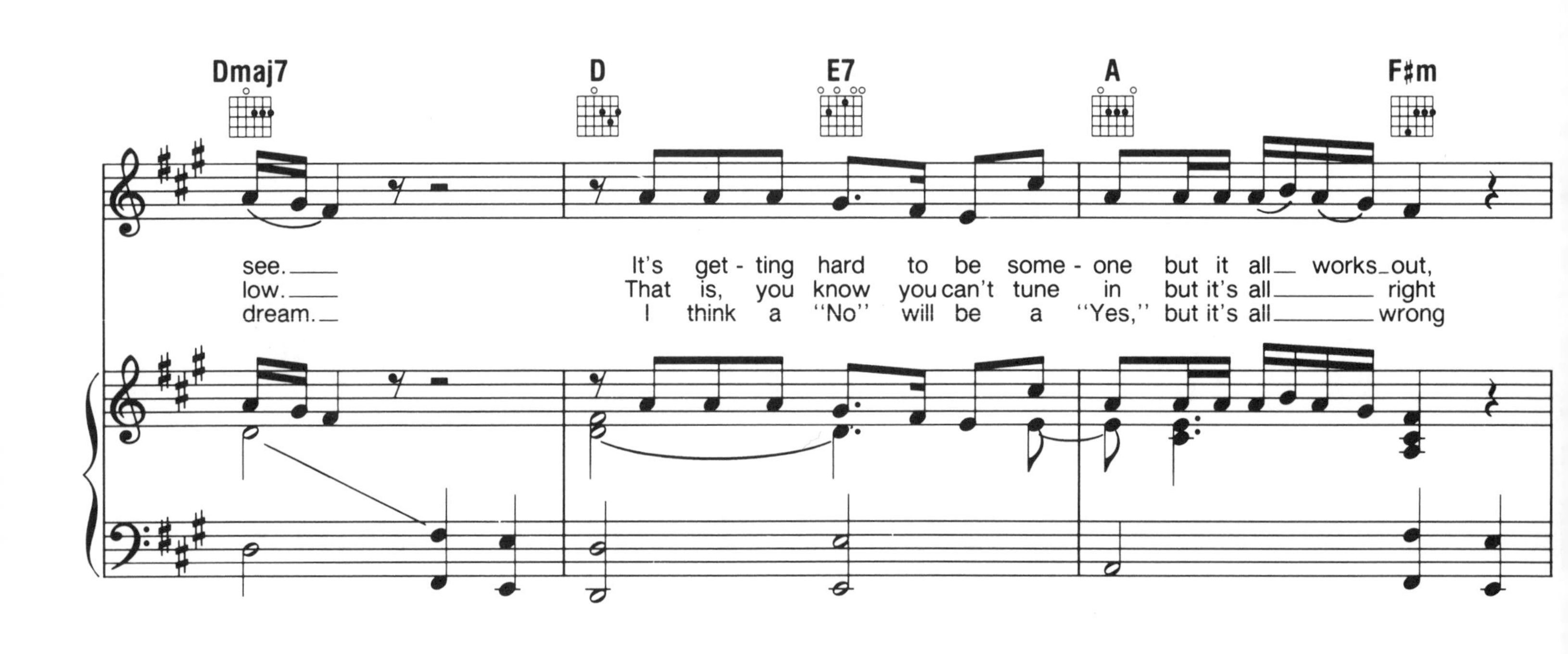
Dmaj7
D
E7
A
F#m
see. It's get - ting hard to be some - one but it all works out,
low. That is, you know you can't tune in but it's all right
dream. I think a "No" will be a "Yes," but it's all wrong

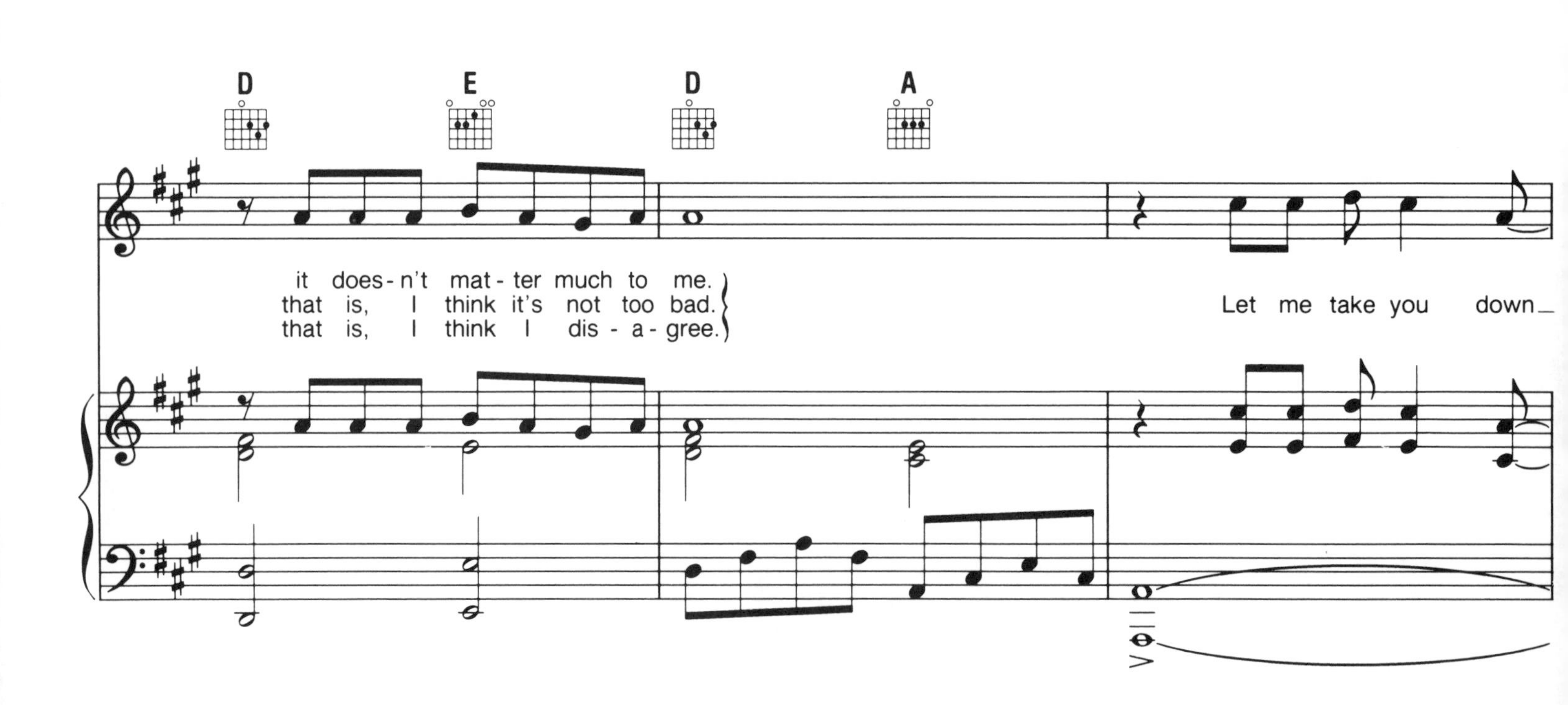
D
E
D
A
it does - n't mat - ter much to me.
that is, I think it's not too bad.
that is, I think I dis - a - gree.
Let me take you down

Em7
C♯dim
'cause I'm go-ing to Straw-ber-ry Fields. Noth-ing is
D
E
F♯
1,2
Dmaj7
A
real, and noth-ing to get hung a-bout... Straw-ber-ry Fields for - ev-er.
3
Dmaj7
A
F♯m
Dmaj7
Straw-ber-ry Fields for - ev-er, Straw-ber-ry Fields for -
A
Dmaj7
E
D
A
ev-er, Straw-ber-ry Fields for - ev-er.

SUITE: JUDY BLUE EYES

Words and Music by
STEPHEN STILLS

A7sus
E
D/A
A
Some - times it hurts so bad - ly I
Don't let the past re - mind us of
E
B
E/B
B
E/B
B
A
must cry out loud.
what we are not now.
I am lone - ly.
I am not dream - ing.
E
B
A
I am yours, you are mine, you are what you are.
1
A7sus
E
A
You make it hard.
Re -
2
A7sus
You make it

E
hard.
Tear - ing your - self
A
E
B
a - way from me now, you are free
A
E
and I am cry - ing.
This does not

A
E
B
mean I don't love you, I do, that's for - ev - er,
A
yes, and for al - ways.
I am yours,
E
B
A
A7sus
you are mine, you are what you are.
You make it
E
A
E
D/A
hard.
Some - thing in - side is

A
E
E/B
B
tell - ing me that I've got your se - cret. Are you still
A
A7
E
D/A
lis - t'ning? Fear is the lock and
A
E
B
laugh - ter the key to your heart, and I
A
E
B
love you. I am yours, you are mine, you are what

A
A7sus
E
A
you are.
You make it
hard,
and you make it
E
A
E
hard,
and you make it
hard,
A
E
and you make it
hard.

E
F♯m
E
Fri - day eve - ning,
Tues - day morn - ing,
F♯m
E
F♯m/A
E/A
A
Sun - day in the af - ter - noon.
please be gone, I'm tired of you.
A7sus
A
E
What have you got to lose?
1
2
3
Can I

D
A
tell it like it is?
But lis - ten to me ba - by.
D
G/A
A
A7
It's my heart that's a - suf - f'rin'. It's a - dy - in'. And that's what I have to
E
lose.
E
F♯m
E
I've got an an - swer.
Will you come see me

F♯m
E
F♯m/A
E/A
A
I'm going to fly a - way.
Thurs - days and Sat - ur - days?
A7sus
A
E
What have I got to lose?
1
2
E

D/E
E
A/E
Chest - nut - brown canar - y,
ru - by throat - ed spar -
Voic - es of the an - gels,
ring a - round the moon -
Lac - y, lilt - ing lyr - ic,
los - ing love, la - ment -

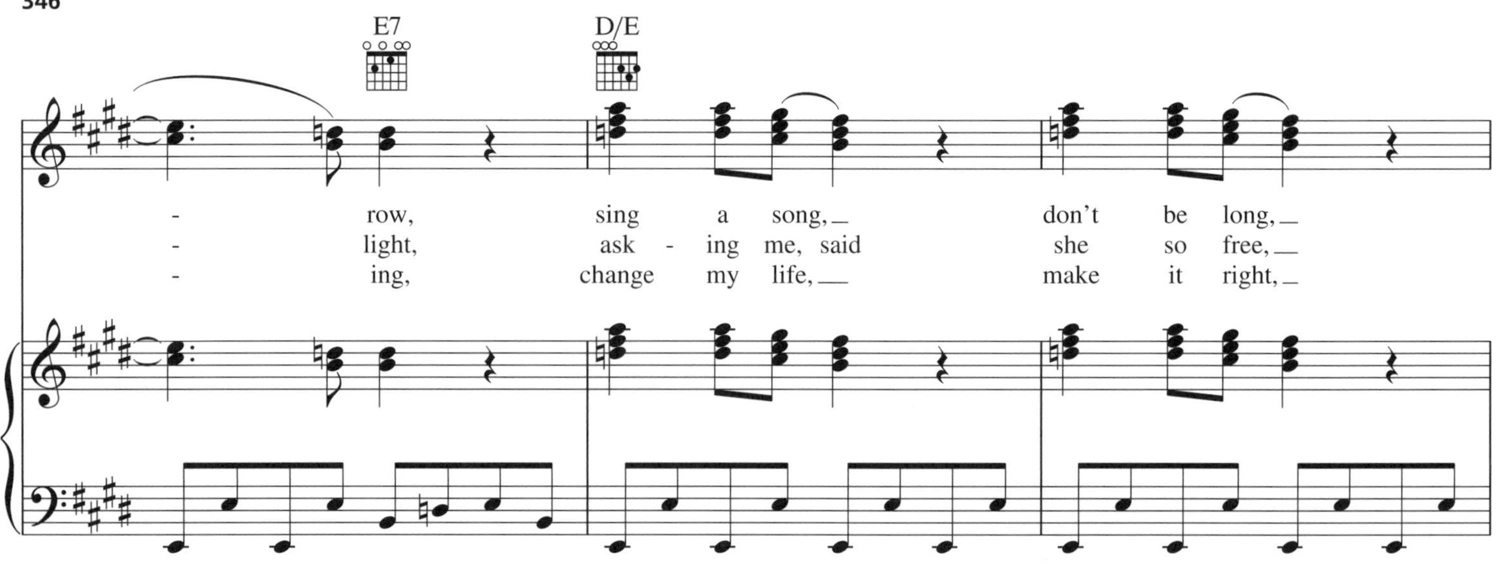
E7
D/E
- row, sing a song, don't be long,
- light, ask - ing me, said she so free,
- ing, change my life, make it right,

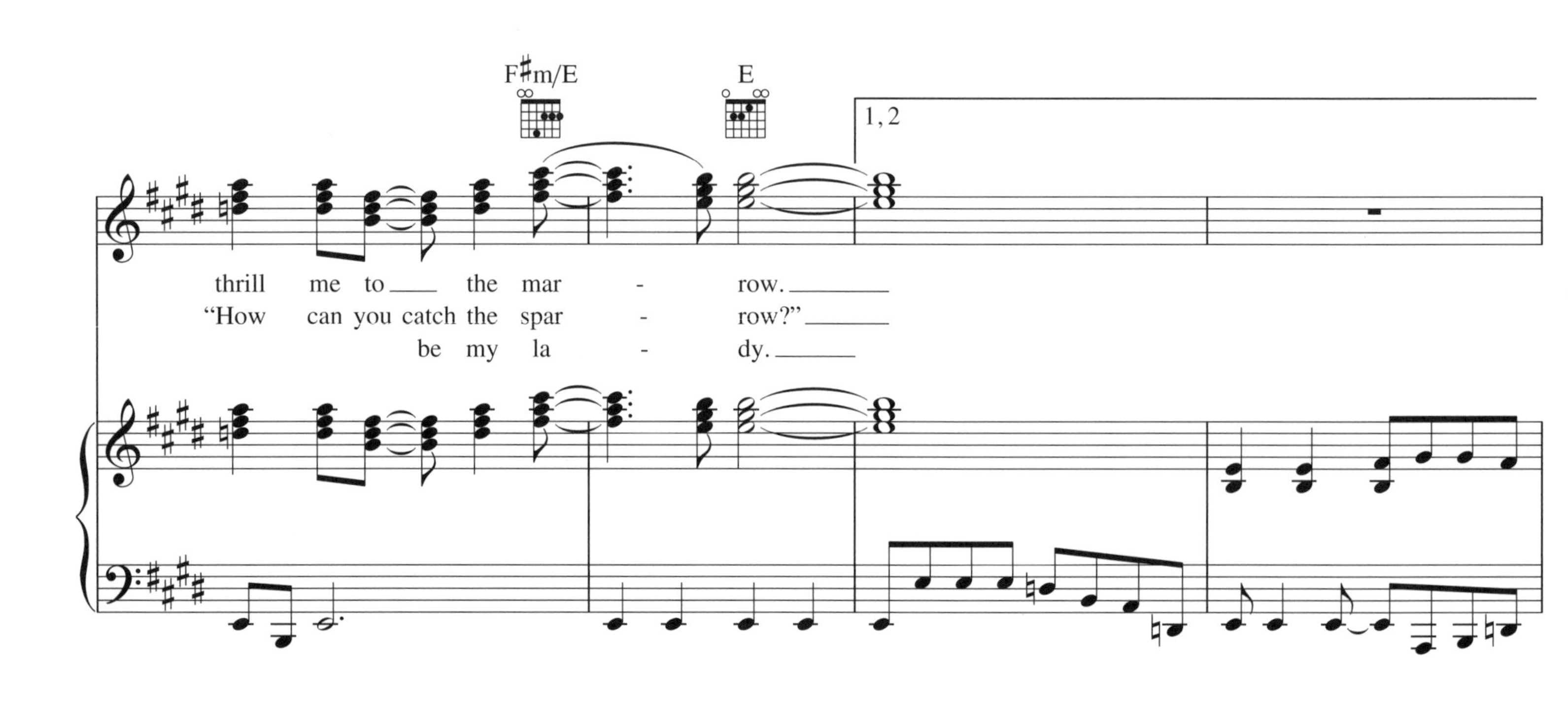
F♯m/E
E
1, 2
thrill me to the mar - row.
"How can you catch the spar - row?"
be my la - dy.

3
D/E
C♯m/E
4fr
Bm/E
A
Bm
F♯m
D
E
1
Do do do do do, do do do do do do, do do do do do, do do do do.

F#m D E A Bm F#m D E A Bm
do do do. Que lin - da me la trai - ga Cu - ba,
sol no tie - ne san - gre a - hi,
F#m D E A Bm F#m D E A Bm
la re - i - na de la Mar - Car - i - be.
y que tris - te que no
F#m D E A Bm F#m D E A Bm
Cie - lo pue - do va - ya. Oh va! Oh va! Do do do do do, do
F#m D E A Bm F#m D E F#m D E
do do do do do, do do do do do, do do do do. do do do.

SUNSHINE OF YOUR LOVE

Words and Music by JACK BRUCE,
PETE BROWN and ERIC CLAPTON

Moderate Rock
mf
D
C
D
no chord
Well, it's get - ting near dawn
I'm with you my love,
when lights close their tired eyes.
the light shin - ing through on you.

D
C
D
no chord
I'll soon be with you my love to
Yes, I'm with you my love. It's the
D
C
D
no chord
give you my dawn sur - prise. I'll
morn - ing and just we two. I'll
G
F
G
no chord
be with you dar - ling soon. I'll
stay with you dar - ling now. I'll
G
F
G
no chord
be with you when the stars are fall - ing.
stay with you 'til my seas are dried up.

D
C
D
no chord
D
C
D
no chord
A
C
G
I've been wait - ing so long
A
C
G
A
to be where I'm go - ing in the sun -
C
G
A
1
- shine of your love.

2
no chord
imitate lead
guitar sound
3

A
I've been wait - ing so long
C
G
A
to be where I'm go - ing
C
G
A
in the sun - shine of your love.
C
G
A

SUMMERTIME BLUES

Words and Music by EDDIE COCHRAN
and JERRY CAPEHART

F
time I call my Ba - by, Try to get a date, My Boss says, "No dice, Son, you
F
G7
got - ta woork late." Some - times I won - der what I'm a - gon - na do But there
C
G7
C
F
ain't no cure for the sum - mer - time blues.
G
C
F
G
C
A well my

C
Mom 'n' Pa - pa told me, "Son, you got - ta make some mon - ey,
take two weeks Gon - na have a fine va - ca - tion,
F
G
C
If you want - ta use the car to go a -
I'm gon - na take my prob - lem to the
rid - in' next Sun - day,"
U - nit - ed Na - tions!
F
G
C
Well, I
Well, I
F
did - n't go to work Told the Boss I was sick "Now you
call my Con - gress - man and He said quote "I'd

can't use the car 'cause you did - n't work a lick"
like to help you, Son, but you're too young to vote"
F
G7
C
Some-times I won-der what I'm a - gon - na do But there ain't no cure for the
G7
C
sum - mer - times blues.
2
F
G
C
I'm gon - na
3
F
G
C
F
G
C

SUPERSTITION

Words and Music by
STEVIE WONDER

(1., 3.) Thir - teen month old ba - by broke the look - ing glass.
(2.) Keep me in a day - dream. Keep me go - in' strong.
Sev - en years of bad luck. The good things in your past.
You don't wan - na save me. Sad is my song.

When you be - lieve
in things that you don't un - der - stand then you suf - fer.
Bb7
Cb7b5
Bb7
A7b5
Ab7
4fr
To Coda
N.C.
Ebm
Su-per - sti - tion ain't the way.
1
2
Ooh, ver - y su - per - sti -

B♭7
C♭7♭5
B♭7
A7♭5
A♭7
4fr
N.C.
E♭m
D.S. al Coda
Ver - y su - per - sti -
CODA
N.C.
E♭m
Su - per - sti - tion ain't the way.
(vocal 1st time only)
Repeat and Fade
Optional Ending

TANGLED UP IN BLUE

Words and Music by
BOB DYLAN

Moderately
A
Asus
mf
G/A
3fr
D
1. Early one mornin' the sun was shinin', I was layin' in bed,
2. She was married when we first met, soon to be divorced.
3. I had a job in the great North woods, workin' as a cook for a spell. But I
4.-7. (See additional lyrics)
8. Instrumental
wond'rin' if she's changed at all, if her hair was still red.
I helped her out of a jam, I guess, but I used a little too much force. We
never did like it all that much and one day the axe just fell. So I

A
G/A
3fr
A
G/A
3fr
Her folks, they said our lives to-geth - er sure was gon-na be rough. They
drove that car as far as we could, a - ban - doned it out west.
drift - ed down to New Or - leans. I was luck - y to be em - ployed,
A
G/A
3fr
D
nev - er did like Ma - ma's home - made dress, Pa - pa's bank book was - n't big e - nough. And
Split up on the docks that night, both a - gree - ing it was best. As
work-in' for a while on a fish - in' boat right out - side of Del - a - croix.
E
F♯m
A
D
I was stand - in' on the side of the road, rain fall - in' on my shoes,
she turned a - round to look at me, as I was walk - in' a - way,
But all the while, I was a - lone, the past was close be - hind.
E
F♯m
A
D
head - ing out for the east coast, Lord knows I've paid some dues get - tin' through.
I heard her say o - ver my shoul - der we'll meet a - gain some - day on the av - e - nue.
I seen a lot of wom - en, but she nev - er 'scaped my mind and I just grew

E
1-7
G
D
Tang - led up in blue.
tang - led up in blue.
A
Asus
A
Asus
A
Asus
A
Asus
8
G
D
A

Additional Lyrics

4. She was working in topless place
   And I stopped in for a beer.
   I just kept looking at the side of her face
   In the spotlight so clear.
   And later on when the crowd thinned out
   I was just about to do the same.
   She was standing there in back of my chair,
   Said to me, "Don't I know your name?"
   I muttered something underneath my breath.
   She studied the lines on my face.
   I must admit I felt a little uneasy
   When she bent down to tie the laces of my shoe,
   Tangled up in blue.

5. She lit a burner on the stove
   And offered me a pipe.
   "I thought you'd never say hello," she said.
   "You look like the silent type."
   Then she opened up a book of poems
   And handed it to me,
   Written by an Italian poet
   From the thirteenth century.
   And every one of them words rang true
   And glowed like burning coal,
   Pourin' off of every page
   Like it was written in my soul,
   From me to you,
   Tangled up in blue.

6. I lived with them on Montague Street
   In a basement down the stairs.
   There was music in the cafes at night
   And revolution in the air.
   Then he started in the dealing in slaves
   And something inside of him died.
   She had to sell everything she owned
   And froze up inside.
   And when finally the bottom finally fell out
   I became withdrawn.
   The only thing I knew how to do
   Was to keep on keeping on,
   Like a bird that flew
   Tangled up in blue.

7. So now I'm going back again.
   I got to get to her somehow.
   All the people we used to know,
   They're an illusion to me now.
   Some are mathematicians,
   Some are carpenter's wives.
   Don't know how it all got started,
   I don't know what they do with their lives.
   But me, I'm still on the road
   Headin' for another joint.
   We always did feel the same,
   We just saw it from a different point of view,
   Tangled up in blue.

THAT'LL BE THE DAY

Words and Music by JERRY ALLISON,
NORMAN PETTY and BUDDY HOLLY

Bb7
Eb
you make me cry, Ah, you say you're gon-na leave, you know it's a lie, 'cause
Bb
Tacet
To Coda
F7
Bb
Bb7
Eb
That-'ll Be The Day when I die. Well, When Cu-pid shot his dart,
mf
Bb
Bb7
Eb
Edim
F7
Bb
Bb7
Eb
He shot it at your heart, So if we ev-er part and I leave you, You say you told me an' you
Bb
C7
C7-5
F
C9
F7
Bb7+5
D.S. al Coda
told me bold-ly, That some day, well, I'll be through. Well,
CODA
F7
Bb
when I die.

THUNDER ROAD

Words and Music by
BRUCE SPRINGSTEEN

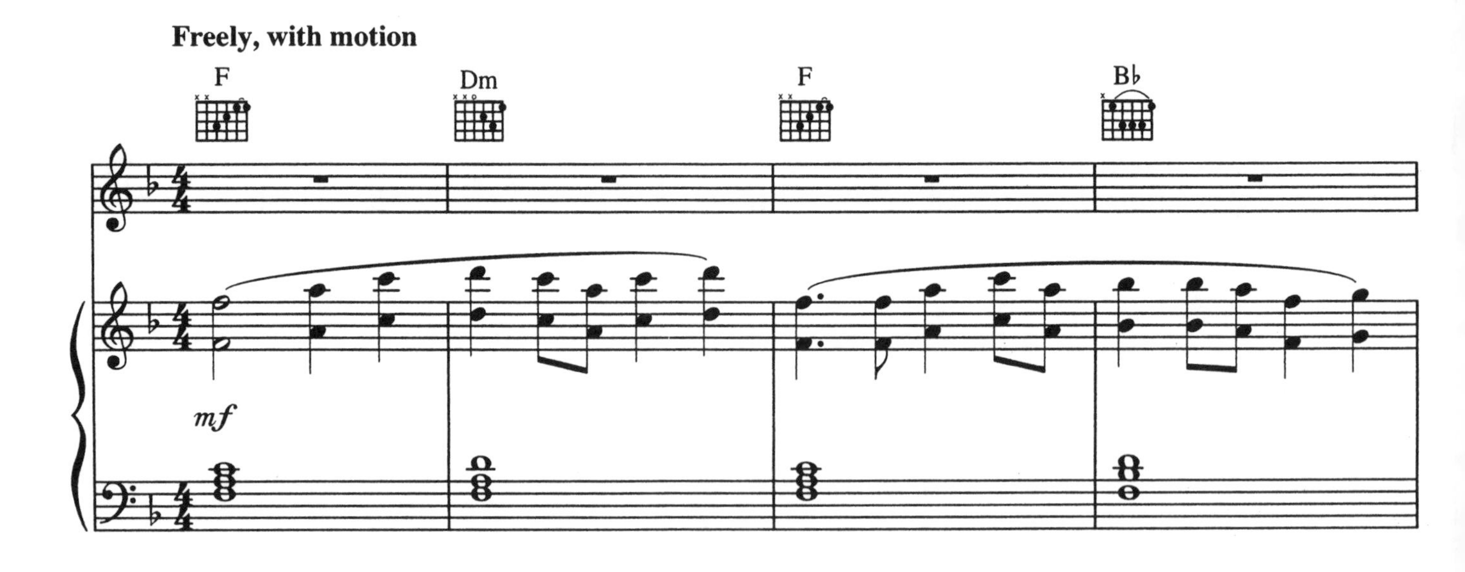

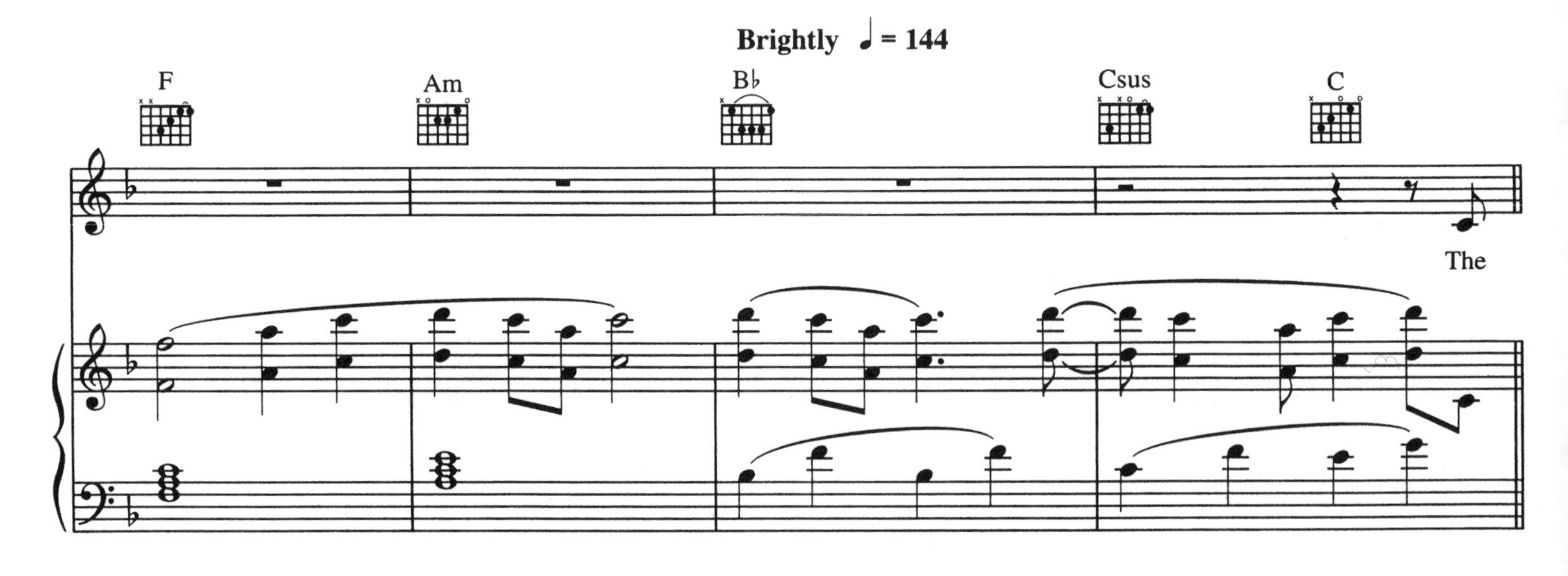

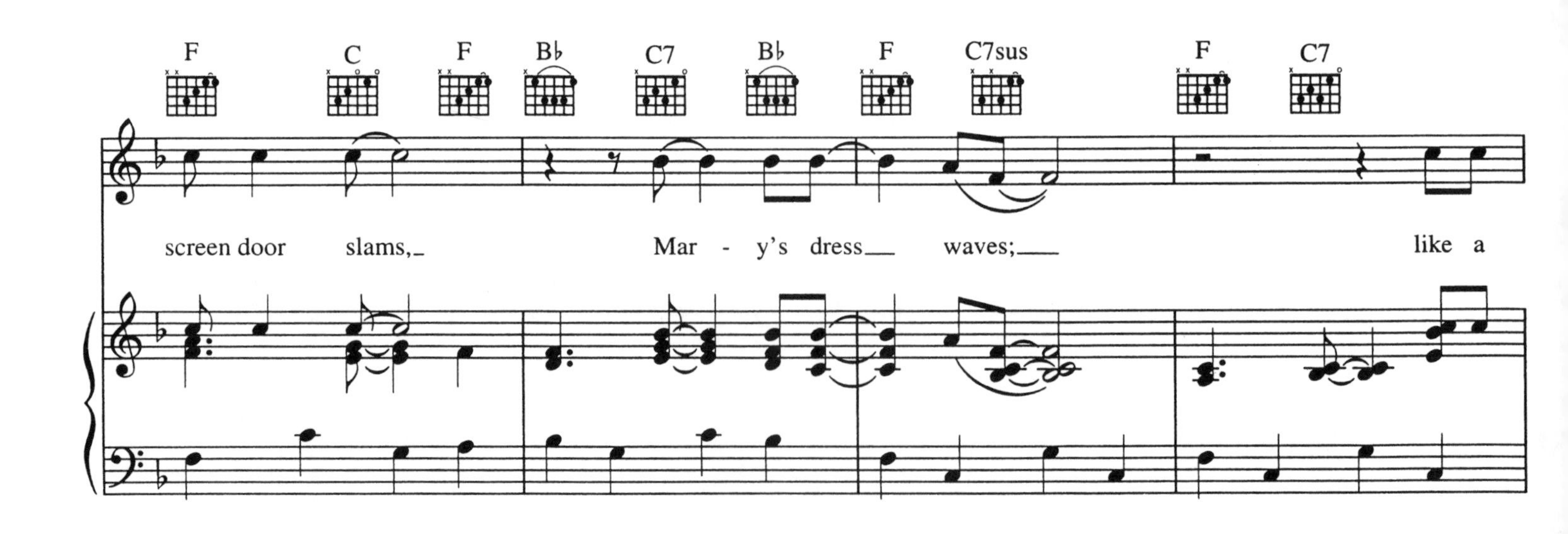

F C7 F C Bb
vi-sion she danc - es a - cross the porch as the ra - di - o plays. Roy
C7 Bb/D C Bb/D C/E F C/E F Bb
Or - bi - son's sing - ing for the lone - ly. Hey, that's me, and I want you on - ly. Don't turn me
Fsus Bb/D F C/E Dm C Bb C C7
home a - gain, I just can't face my - self a - lone a - gain. Don't
F C7 F Bb C7 F C7
run back in - side, dar - ling, you know just what I'm here for.

F C7 F C7 F C
So you're scared and you're think-ing that may - be we ain't that
B♭ C7 B♭/D
young an - y - more. Show a lit - tle faith, there's mag - ic in the
C7 B♭/D C7/E F C7/G F/A B♭ F B♭ F/A C7/G
night. You ain't a beau-ty, but hey, you're al - right. Oh, and
F C7 Gm7 C7
that's al - right with me. You can

F (With a moving beat)
Dm
F
hide 'neath your cov - ers and stud - y your pain, make cross - es from your lov - ers, throw
B♭
F
Am
ros - es in the rain, waste your sum - mer, pray - ing in vain for a
B♭
Gm7/C
C7
F
sav - ior to rise from these streets. Well now, I'm no he - ro, that's un - der -
Dm
F
B♭
C7
stood. All the re - demp - tion I can of - fer, girl, is be - neath this dirt - y hood,

F
Dm
B♭
C7
with a chance to make it good some - how. Hey, what else can we do now, ex - cept
F
B♭
F
roll down the win-dow and let the wind blow back your hair.
f
Am
Well, the night's bust-ing o - pen, these two lanes will take us
B♭
C7
an - y - where. We got one last chance to make it real. To

F
B♭
F
trade in these wings on some wheels.
Climb in back, heav - en's wait-ing down on
C7
F
Dm
the tracks.
Oh, come take my hand,
F
B♭
F
Am
rid-ing out to-night to case the prom - ised land.
Oh, Thun - der Road,
B♭
C7
F
Dm
oh, Thun-der Road,
oh, Thun-der Road,
ly-ing out there like a kill-er in the sun.

F
B♭
F
Am
3
Hey, I know it's late, we can make it if we run. Oh, Thun-der Road, sit
B♭
C7
F
Gm7
F/A
B♭
tight, take hold, Thun-der Road. Well, I got
C7
F
B♭/F
F
B♭/F
F
this gui-tar, and I learned how to make it talk. And my
Dm
B♭maj7
C
car's out back, if you're read-y to take that long walk from your

B♭
C
Am
Dm
front porch to my front seat. The door's o - pen but the ride ain't free, and
B♭
B♭/A
Gm7
B♭/F
C7
I know you're lone - ly for words that I ain't spo - ken, but to - night we'll be free. All the
F
B♭
prom-is - es - 'll be bro - ken. There were ghosts in the eyes of all the boys you
F
sent a - way. They haunt this dust - y beach road in the

Am
B♭
skel-e-ton frames_ of burned out Chev - ro - lets.__ They scream your name at night in the street,_
C
F
B♭
Am
__ your grad-u - a-tion gown lies in rags at their__ feet. And in the lone - ly cool_ be-fore
B♭
3
dawn,____ you hear their en-gines roar - ing on.___ But when you
Gm
F
Em7(♭5)
Dm
C
B♭
Am
Gm
B♭
get to the porch, they're gone on the wind._ So, Mar - y climb

Gm
B♭
in.
It's a town full of los - ers,
I'm
C7
F
pull-ing out of here to win.
gliss.
(Drums)
F
C
F
B♭
Instrumental Solo
F
C
B♭
C
Repeat and fade

THE TWIST

Words and Music by
HANK BALLARD

C7
G
G7
and go like this: Ee oh
tear the house down. Ee oh Twist,
and she knows how to Twist. Ee oh
f
ba - by, ba - by, Twist, ('round and a - round and a - round and a)- Just,
C7
G
D7
just like this, ('round and a - round) Come on, lit - tle miss,
C7
G
1,2
3
and do The Twist. ('round and a - round.) While Dad - dy is
You should round.)

TWIST AND SHOUT

Words and Music by BERT RUSSELL
and PHIL MEDLEY

Moderately with a beat
D
G
A7
f
Well, shake it up ba - by, now,
- by, now,
- by, now,
(Shake it up ba - by)
Twist and
shout.
(Twist and shout)
Come on, come on, come on, come on,

D
G
A7
D
G
ba - by now,
Come on and work it on out.
(Come on ba - by)
(Work it on out)
A7
D
G
1. Well, work it on out,
2,3. You know you twist, lit - tle girl,
(Work it on out)
(Twist lit - tle girl)
A7
D
G
A7
You know you look so good.
You know you twist so fine.
(Look so good)
(Twist so fine)
You know you got me
Come on and twist a lit - tle
D
G
A7
go - in' now,
clos - er now,
(Got me goin')
(Twist a lit - tle clos - er)
Just like I knew you would.
And let me know that you're

D
G
To Coda
1 A7
2 A7
(Like I knew you would)
Well, shake it up ba -
mine. (Let me know you're mine)
D
G
A
G
A
D
G
A
G
A
D
G
A
G
A
D
G
A
G
A
Ah
Ah

A7
D.S. al Coda
Ah
Ah
Ah
Shake it up ba -
CODA
A7
D
G
Well, shake it, shake it, shake it, ba - by, now,
(Shake it up ba -
A7
D
G
A
Well, shake it, shake it, shake it, ba - by now.
- by.)
(Shake it up, ba - by.)
Ah
A7
D
Dmaj9
Ah
Ah
Ah

WALK THIS WAY

Words and Music by STEVEN TYLER
and JOE PERRY

ain't seen noth in' till you're down on a muf-fin, then you're
"Hey, did - dle, did - dle," with your kit - ty in the mid - dle of the
three young la - dies in the school gym lock - er when I
"Hey, did - dle, did - dle," with your kit - ty in the mid - dle of the
sure to be a chang-in' your ways." I meet a
swing like you did - n't care. So I
no - ticed they was look - in' at me. I was a
swing like you did - n't care. So I
cheer - lead - er, was a real young bleed - er, oh, the
took a big chance at the high school dance with a
high school los - er, nev - er made it with a la - dy till the
took a big chance at the high school dance with a
times I could rem - i - nisce; 'cause the
miss - y who was read - y to play. Was it
boys told me some-thin' I missed. Then my
miss - y who was read - y to play. Was it

best things of lov - in' with her sis - ter and her cous - in on - ly
me she was fool - in', 'cause she knew what she was do - in' when I
next door neigh-bor with a daugh-ter had a fa - vor, so I
me she was fool - in', 'cause she knew what she was do - in' when she
1,3
A
start - ed with a lit - tle kiss like this.
knowed love was here to stay
gave her just a lit - tle kiss like this.
told me how to walk this way.
no chord

A
2,4
C
when she told me to
She told me to
walk this way,
F7
1,2,3
walk this way,
4
C
and just gim-me a kiss

A
To Coda
like
this!
no chord
A
D.S. al Coda
CODA
no chord
Repeat and Fade

WILD THING

Words and Music by
CHIP TAYLOR

F
Eb
F
Eb
F
WILD THING, I think I love you.
WILD THING, I think you move me.
But I wan - na know
But I wan - na know
for sure.
for sure.
Come on and hold me tight.
Come on and hold me tight.
I love you.
You move me.
C
Bb

F
B♭
C
B♭
F
B♭
WILD THING,
You make my heart sing.
C
B♭
F
B♭
C
B♭
You make eve - ry - thing groov - y.
F
B♭
C
Repeat and Fade
WILD THING.

WE ARE THE CHAMPIONS

Words and Music by
FREDDIE MERCURY

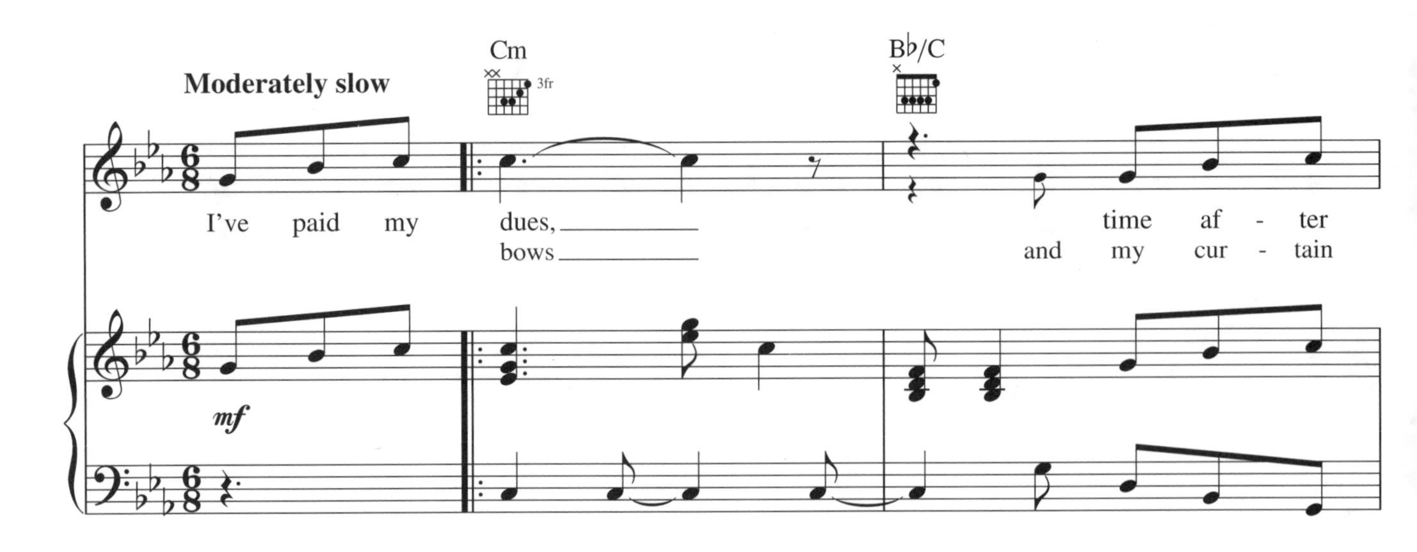

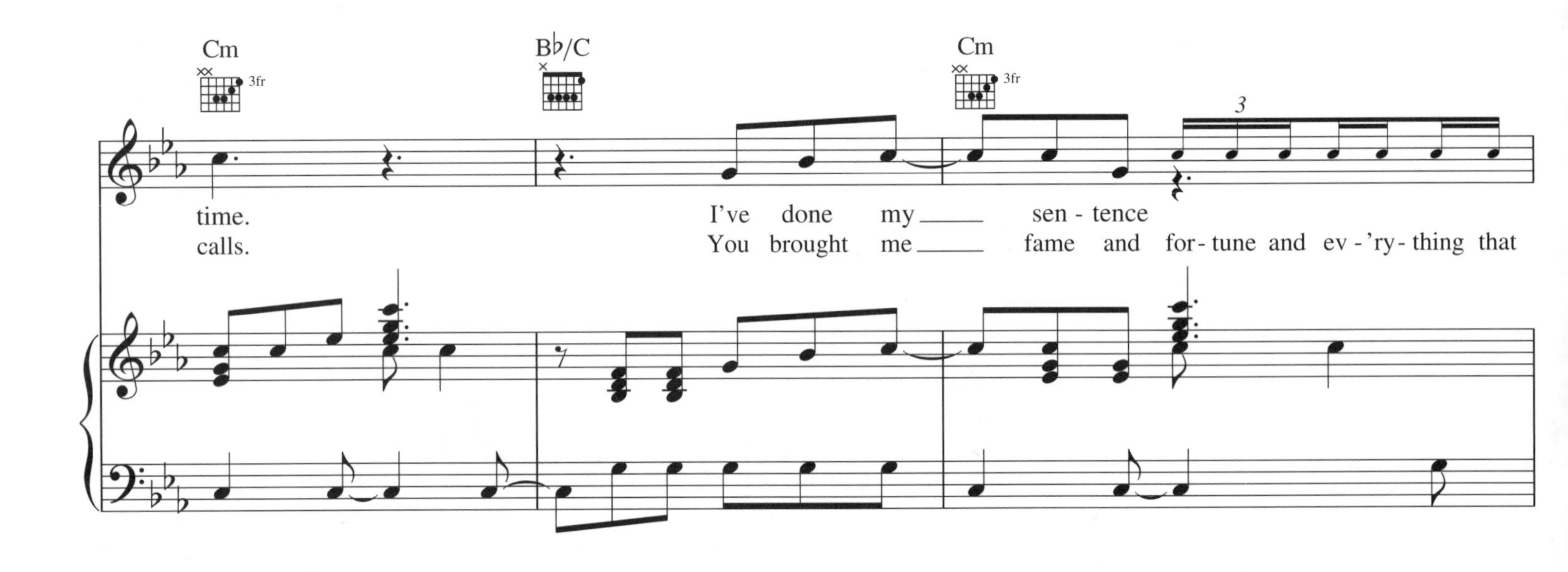

B♭/C
E♭
And bad mis - takes,
But it's been no bed of ros - es,
A♭
E♭
A♭
I've made a few.
no pleas - ure cruise.
I've had my
I con - sid - er it a
E♭
B♭/D
Cm
F
share of sand kicked in my face but I've come
chal - lenge be - fore the whole hu - man race and I ain't gon - na
B♭
C
through.
lose.
And I need to go on, and on, and on, and on.

F
Am7
Dm7
We are the cham - pions my friend.
(D.S.) world.
Bb
C
F
Am7
And we'll keep on fight - ing till the
Bb
F#dim7
Gm
3fr
end.
We are the
C/G
Bbdim7
cham - pions.
We are the cham - pions.

F
Gm7
3fr
A♭6
3fr
To Coda
B♭7
No time for los - ers, 'cause we are the cham - pions
1
C7sus
Fm
B♭/F
Fm
of the world.
B♭/F
Fm
C7sus
I've tak - en my
2
C7sus
D.S. al Coda
of the
CODA
B♭7
C7sus
cham - pions.

WE'VE ONLY JUST BEGUN

Words and Music by ROGER NICHOLS
and PAUL WILLIAMS

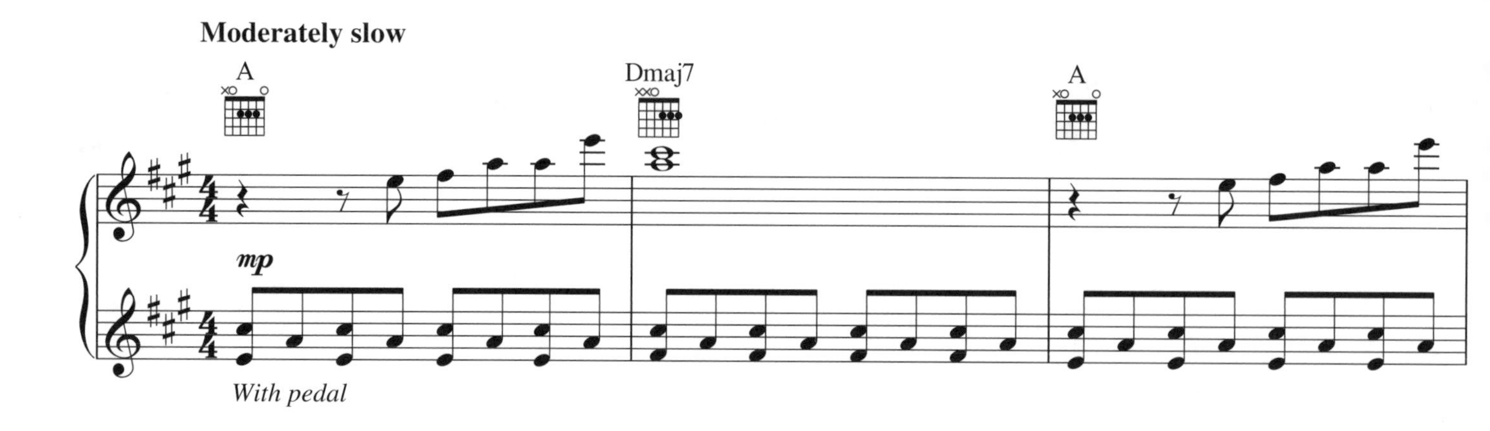
Moderately slow
A
Dmaj7
A
mp
With pedal

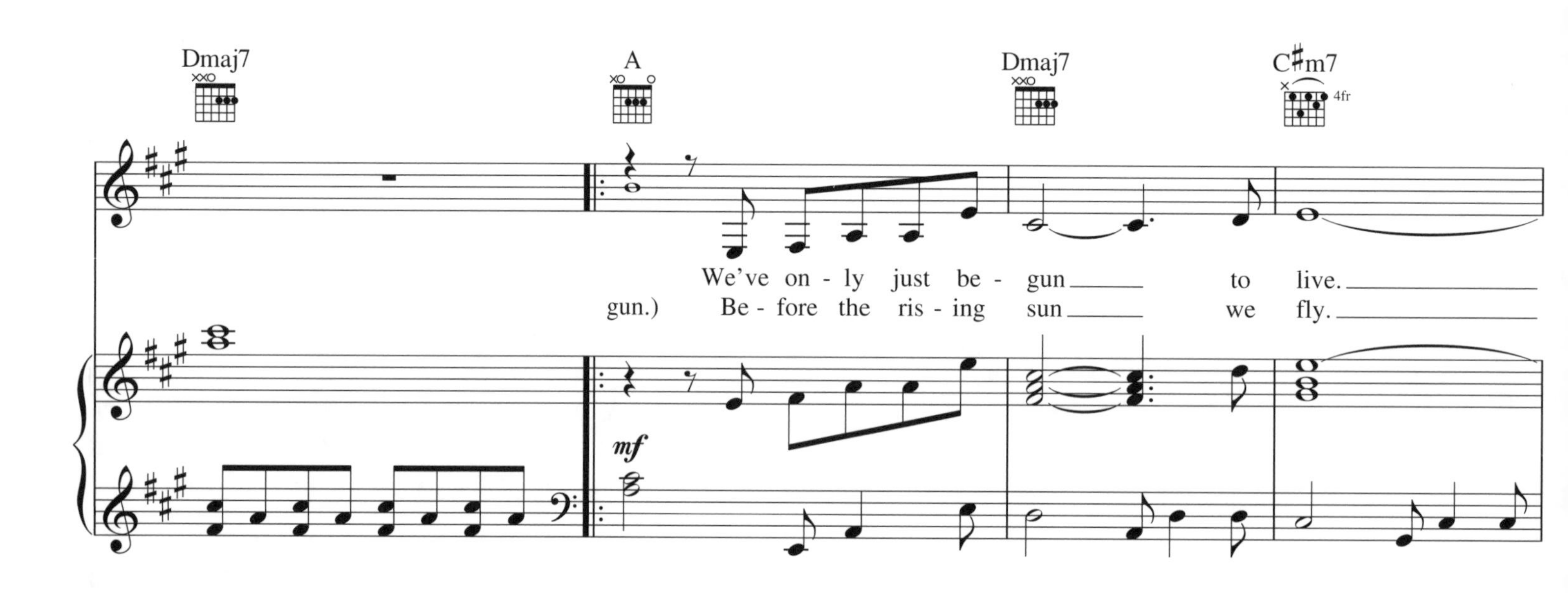
Dmaj7
A
Dmaj7
C#m7
4fr
We've on - ly just be - gun to live.
gun.) Be - fore the ris - ing sun we fly.
mf

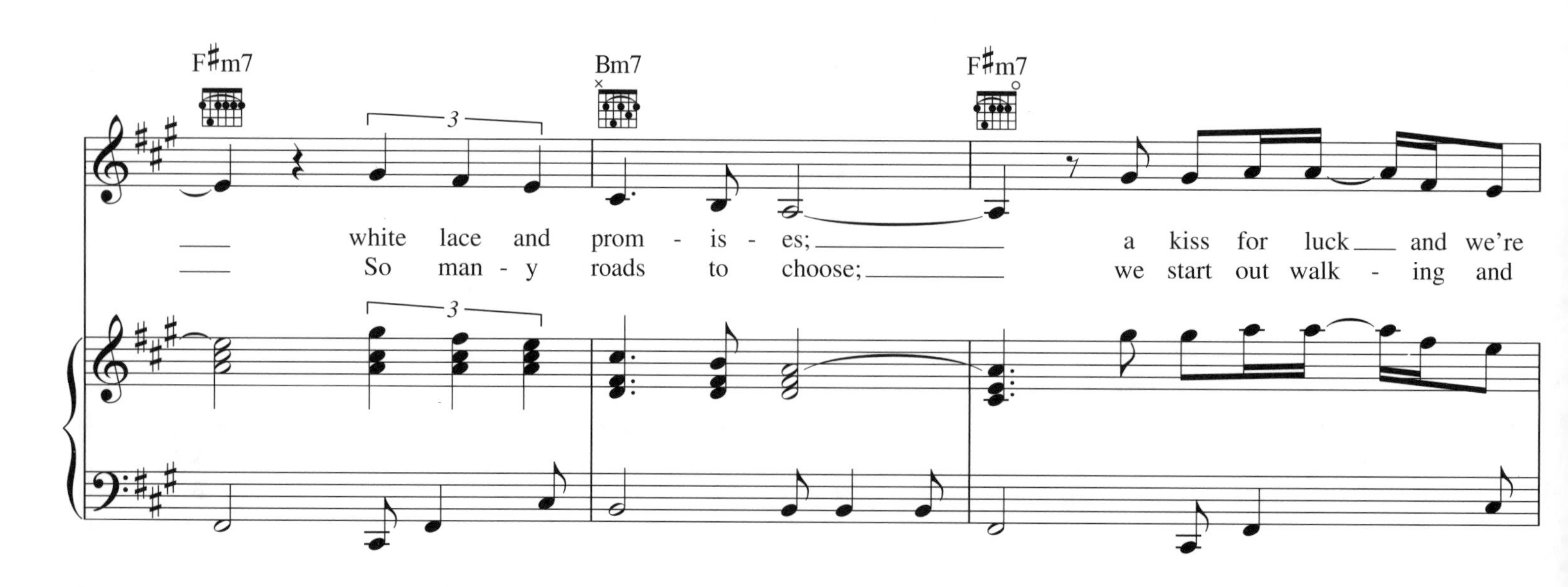
F#m7
Bm7
F#m7
3
white lace and prom - is - es; a kiss for luck and we're
So man - y roads to choose; we start out walk - ing and

Bm7
Bm7/E
E
Bm7/E
A
Dmaj7
on our way,
(We've on - ly be -
learn to run.
(And yes, we've just be - gun.)
A
Dmaj7
E
F♯
Bmaj7
F♯
Bmaj7
Shar - ing hor - i - zons that are new to us,
F♯
Bmaj7
F♯
Bmaj7
B♭
E♭maj7
watch - ing the signs a - long the way.
Talk - ing it o - ver, just the
To Coda
B♭
E♭maj7
B♭
E♭maj7
E7sus
E
two of us,
work - ing to - geth - er day to day,
to - geth - er.

A(add2)
Dmaj7
C#m7
4fr
And when the eve - ning comes we smile.
F#m7
Bm7
F#m7
3
So much of life a - head, we'll find a place where there's
D.S. al Coda
Bm7
E
Bm7/E
A
Dmaj7
A
Dmaj7
E
room to grow. (And yes, we've just be - gun.)
CODA
E
A
geth - er, to - geth - er. And when the eve - ning

Dmaj7
C♯m7
4fr
F♯m7
3
comes we smile. So much of
Bm7
F♯m7
Bm7
life a - head, we'll find a place where there's room to grow.
E
A
Dmaj7
And yes, we've just be - gun.
Amaj7
Dmaj7
C♯

WHAT'D I SAY

Words and Music by
RAY CHARLES

F7
C7
Bb7
F7
hey,
hey,
right
All
All
You don't do
right, now.
right, now.
right.
3
F
Play 3 times
Tell me what I'd
say?
know,
Tell me what I'd
I
say
wan-na
right now?
know.
Bb7
F
Tell me what'd I
Ba-by, I
say?
wan-na
know right now.
Tell me what'd I
Yes, I wan-na
say?
know.
C7
Bb7
F
Tell me what'd I
Hon-ey I
say?
wan-na
know.
Tell me what'd I
Yes, I wan-na
say?
know.

1
2
Yes, I wan - na
Hey, (hey) Ho,
Hey, (hey) Ho,
Huh, (huh) Ho,
(ho) Hey, (hey) Ho, (ho) Hey, (hey) Ho, (ho) Hey, Sing me one more
(ho) Hey, (hey) Ho, (ho) Hey, (hey) Ho, (ho) Hey, Make me feel so
(ho) Huh, (huh) Ho, (ho) Huh, (huh) Ho, (ho) Huh, Ba - by it's all
Bb7
time, Sing me one more time, Sing me one more time.
good, Make me feel so good, Make me feel so good right now.
right, Ba - by, it's all right, right now, Ba - by it's all right.
F
C7
Sing me one more time, Sing me one more time,
Make me feel so good, Make me feel so good,
Ba - by it's all right, Ba - by it's all right,

Bb7
F
1, 2
3
Sing me one more time.
Make me feel so good.
Ba - by it's all right.
Come on twist that thing,
right,
Come on, twist that thing,
Well, I feel all right,
Bb7
Keep a twist - in' that thing,
Well, I feel all right,
F
C7
Keep a twist - in' that thing,
Well, I feel all right,
Keep a twist - in' that thing,
Well I feel all right,
Bb7
F
1
2
F9
Keep a twist - in' that thing.
Well I feel all right.
Make me feel all

WHAT'S GOING ON

Words and Music by MARVIN GAYE,
AL CLEVELAND and RENALDO BENSON

Moderately
Emaj7
mf

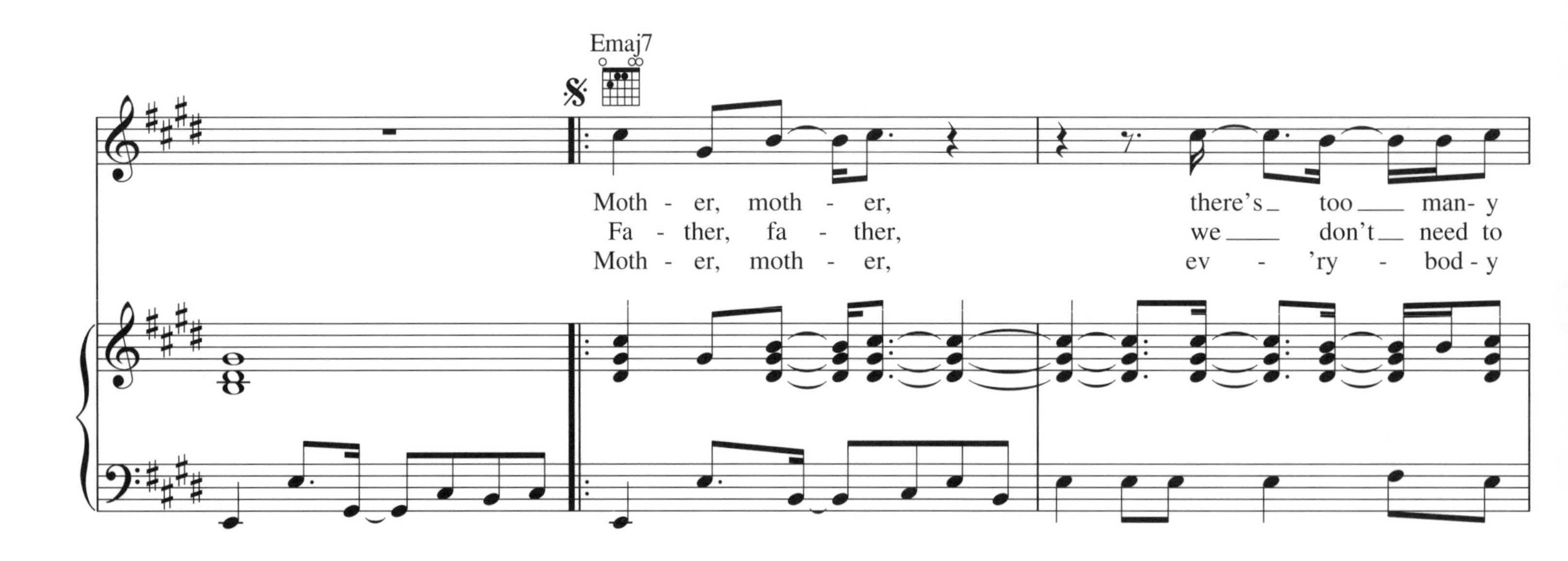
Emaj7
Moth - er, moth - er, there's too man - y
Fa - ther, fa - ther, we don't need to
Moth - er, moth - er, ev - 'ry - bod - y

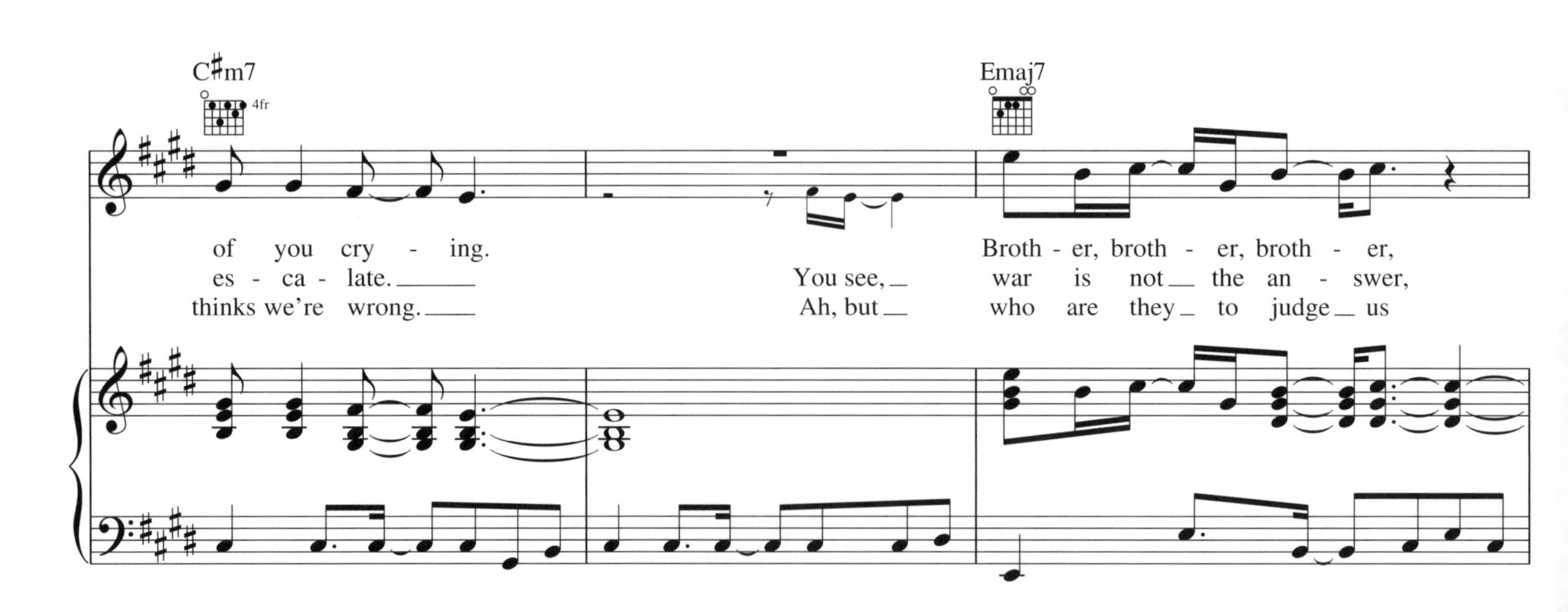
C#m7
4fr
Emaj7
of you cry - ing. Broth - er, broth - er, broth - er,
es - ca - late. You see, war is not the an - swer,
thinks we're wrong. Ah, but who are they to judge us

C♯m7
4fr
there's far too man - y of you dy - ing.
for on - ly love can con - quer hate.
sim - ply 'cause our hair is long.
F♯m7
You know we've got to find a way to bring some
You know we've got to find a way to bring some
Ah, you know we've got to find a way to bring some un - der -
3
1
F♯m7/B
B7(add13)
lov - in' here to - day, yeah.
2, 3
F♯m7/B
lov - in' here to - day, oh.
stand - ing here to - day, oh.
B7(add13)
F♯m7
F♯m7/B
Pick - et lines and pick - et signs don't

F#m7
F#m7/B
pun - ish me with bru - tal - i - ty.
F#m7
F#m7/B
Talk to me so you can see, oh, what's
Emaj7
C#m7
4fr
go - ing on, what's go - ing on, yeah, what's
To Coda
Emaj7
C#m7
4fr
go - ing on, oh, what's go - ing on. Ah, ah, ah,

Am9
ah, ah.
I, yi, yi, yi, yi, yi, yi, ya, ya, ya, ya.
I, yi, yi, yi, yi, yi, ya, ya, ya, ya, ya.

A/B
Be, doot, de doot; Be, be, be, doot; Be be, be, doot;
D.S. al Coda
Bu, doot, be, be, be, doot; Be be, be, be, be, doot.
CODA
C♯m7
4fr
Am9
go - ing on, ooh, ooh.
I, yi, yi, yi, yi, yi, yi, ya,

ya, ya, ya.
I, yi, yi, yi, yi, yi, ya, ya, ya, ya, ya.
A/B
Be, doot, de, doot; Be, be, be, doot; Be be, be, doot;
Repeat and Fade
Bu, doot, be, be, be, doot; Be, be, be, be, be, doot. Ooh,

WHEN DOVES CRY

Composed by PRINCE

Medium tempo

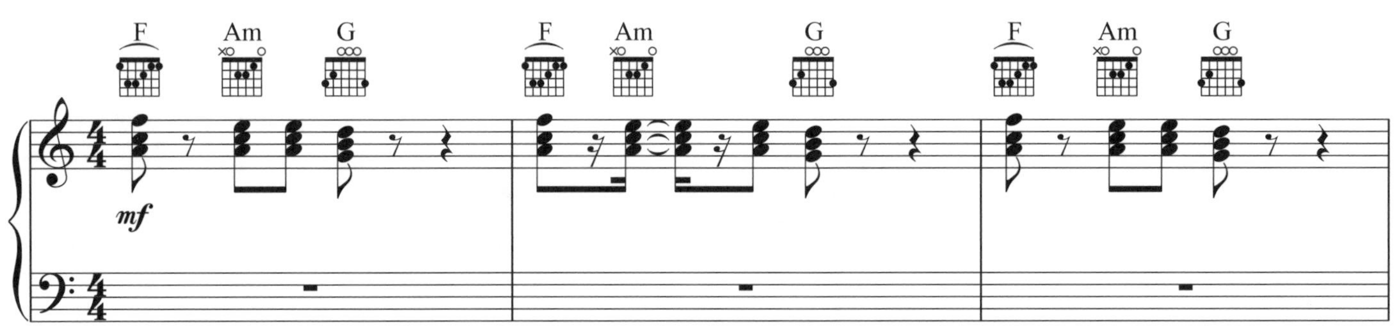
F
Am
G
F
Am
G
F
Am
G
mf

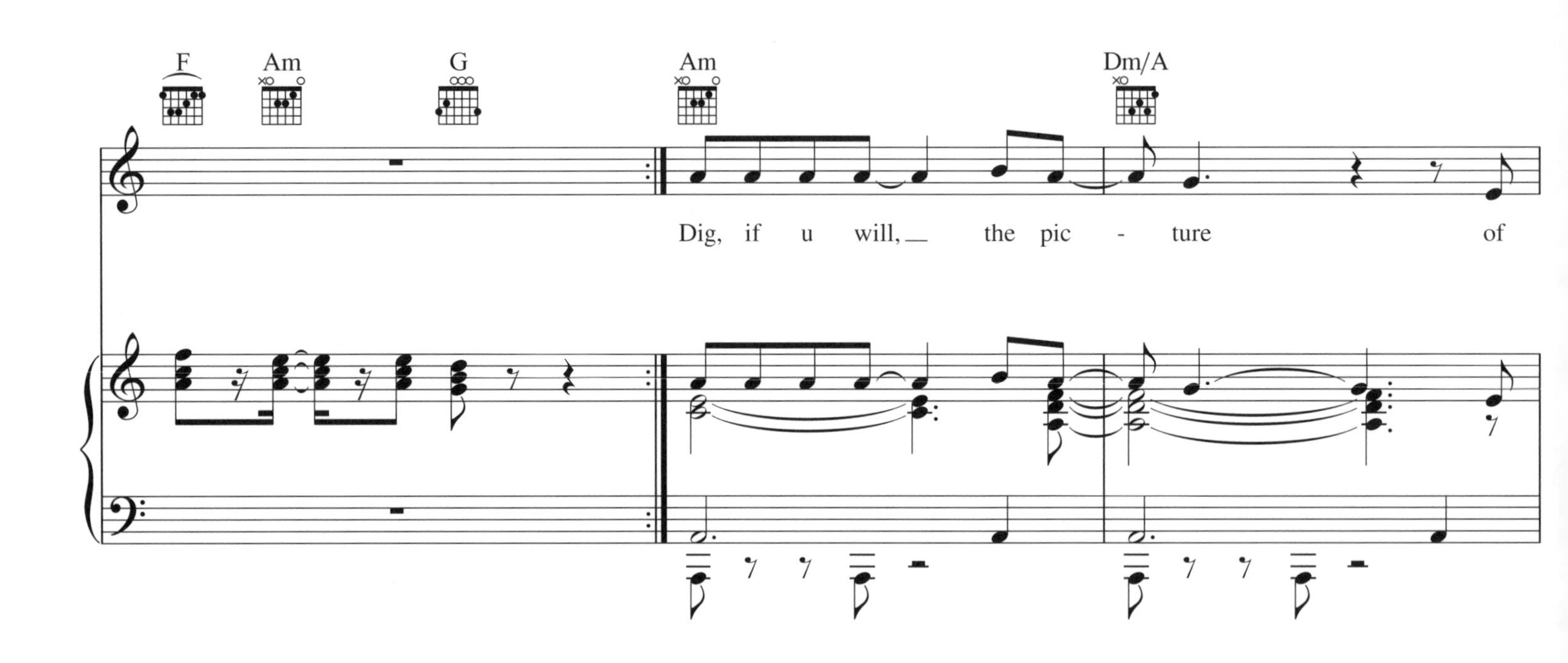
F
Am
G
Am
Dm/A
Dig, if u will, the pic - ture of

G
E7♯5/G♯
E7/G♯
Am
u and I en-gaged in a kiss. The sweat of your bod - y cov -

Dm/A
G
E7♯5/G♯
E7/G♯
- ers me.
Can u, my dar - ling,
can u pic - ture this?
Am
Dm/A
G
Dream, if u can, a court - yard,
an o - cean of vi - 'lets in bloom.
Touch, if u will, my stom - ach.
Feel how it trem - bles in - side.
E7♯5/G♯
E7/G♯
Am
Dm/A
An - i - mals strike cu - ri - ous pos - es.
You've got the but - ter - flies all tied up.
G
E7♯5/G♯
E7/G♯
Am
(Both times:) How can u just leave me stand -
They feel the heat, the heat be - tween me and u.
Don't make me chase u. E - ven doves have pride.

Dm/A
G
E7#5/G#
E7/G#
- ing a - lone in a world that's so cold?
Am
Dm/A
G
May - be I'm just 2 de - mand - ing. May - be I'm just like my
E7#5/G#
E7/G#
Am
Dm/A
fa - ther – 2 bold. May - be you're just like my moth - er.
G
E7#5/G#
E7/G#
Am
She's nev - er sat - is - fied. Why do we scream at each oth -

Dm/A
G
To Coda
E7♯5/G♯
E7/G♯
- er? This is what it sounds like when doves _ cry.
F
Am
G
1
2
D.S. al Coda
CODA
Am
when doves _ cry.

YESTERDAY

Words and Music by JOHN LENNON
and PAUL McCARTNEY

Moderately, with expression

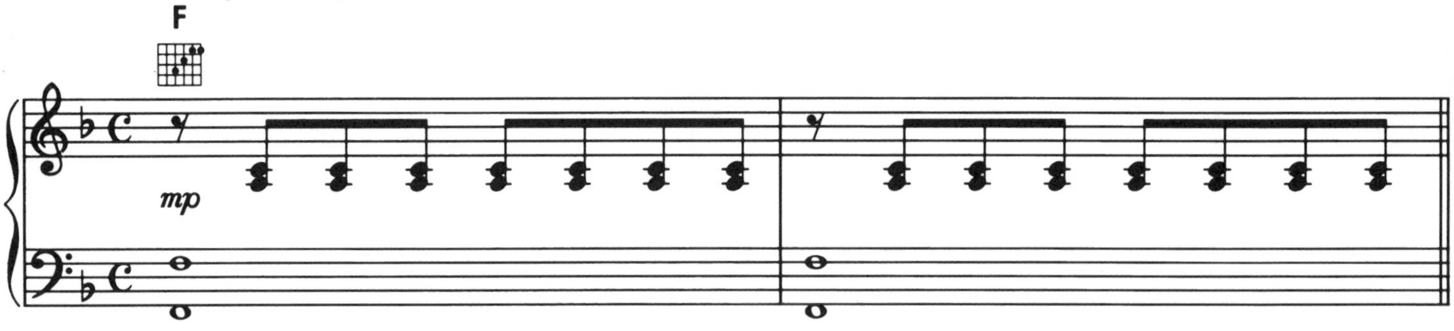

F

mp

F Em A7

Yes- ter- day, all my trou-bles seemed so
Sud-den- ly, I'm not half the man I

Dm Dm/C B♭ C

far a - way, Now it looks as though they're
used to be, There's a sha - dow hang - ing

B♭/F F C/E Dm7 G7 B♭ F
here to stay, oh I be - lieve in yes - ter - day.
o - ver me, oh yes - ter - day came sud - den - ly.
G/A A7 Dm C B♭maj7 Dm/A Gm C7
Why she had to go I don't know, she would - n't say.
F G/A A7
I said
Dm C B♭maj7 Dm/A Gm C F
some - thing wrong, now I long for yes - ter - day.

Em
A7
Yes- ter- day,
love was such an eas - y
Dm
B♭
C
game to play.
Now I need a place to
B♭/F
F
C/E
Dm7
G7
B♭
F
hide a - way,
oh I be- lieve
in yes - ter - day.
F/C
G/B
B♭
F
Mm mm mm mm mm.
rit.

YOU REALLY GOT ME

Words and Music by
RAY DAVIES

F
Eb
F
Eb
F
Eb
F
Eb
so I can't sleep at night
G
F
G
F
G
F
G
F
Yeah you real - ly got me now you got me
G
F
G
F
G
F
G
so I don't know what I'm do - ing
Oh
C
Bb
C
Bb
C
Bb
C
Bb
yeah you real - ly got me now You got me

C
Bb
C
Bb
C
Bb
C
Bb
so I can't sleep at night you real - ly got me You
real - ly got me You real - ly got me
1
2
Oh oh
3
C

YOUR SONG

Words and Music by ELTON JOHN
and BERNIE TAUPIN

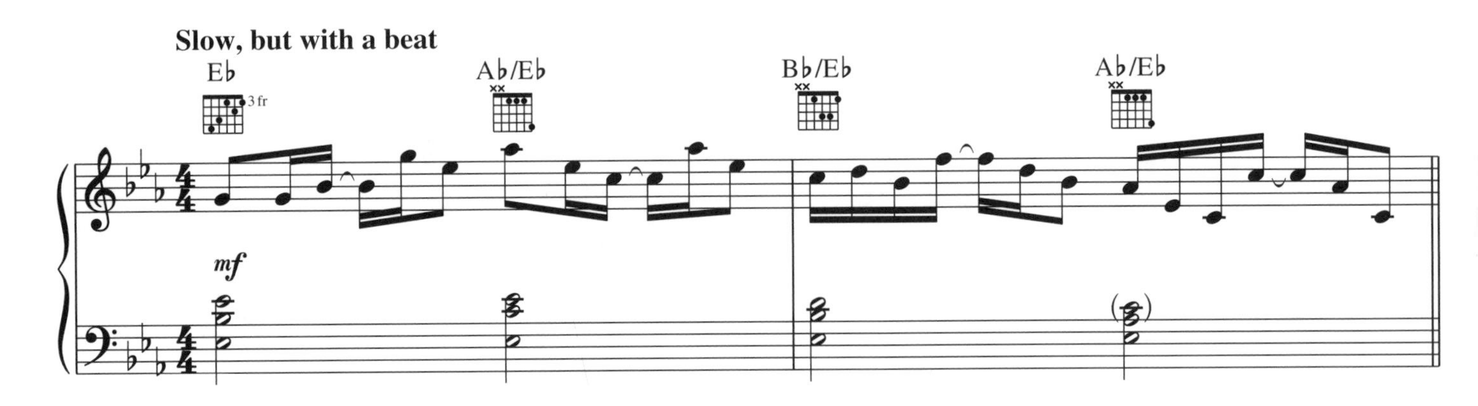
Slow, but with a beat
Eb
Ab/Eb
Bb/Eb
Ab/Eb
3 fr
mf

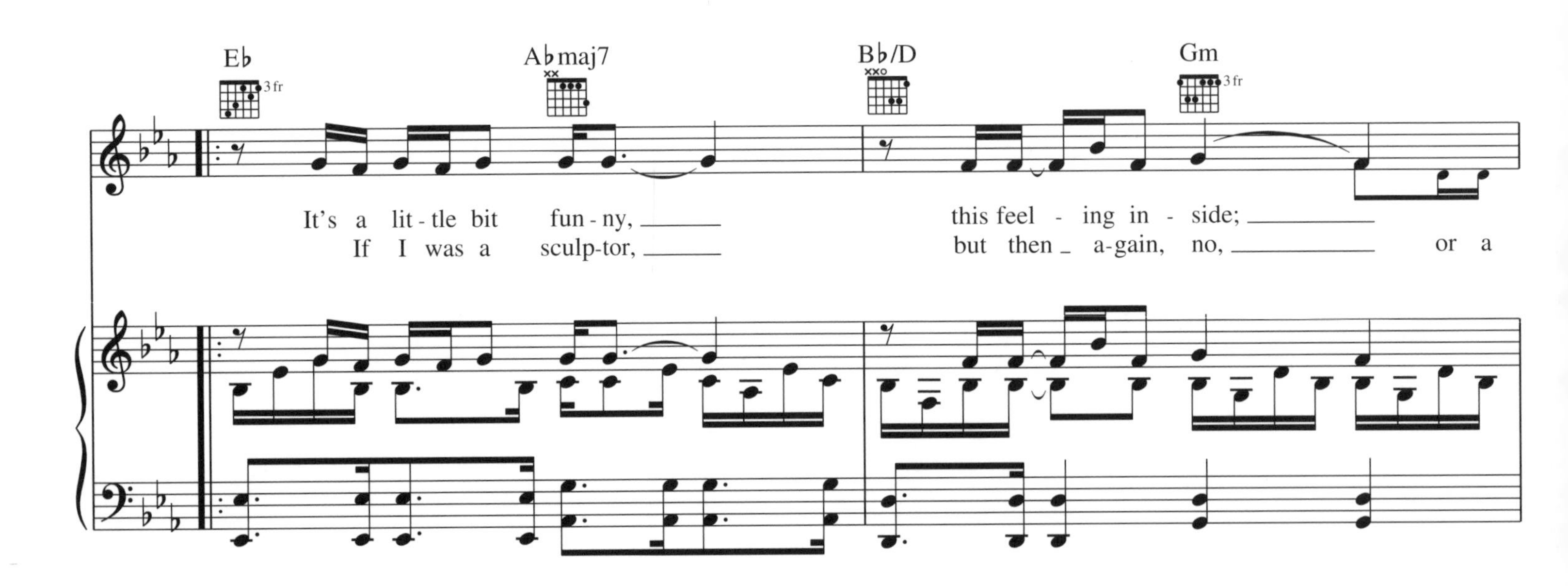
Eb
Abmaj7
Bb/D
Gm
3 fr
It's a lit-tle bit fun-ny, this feel - ing in - side;
If I was a sculp-tor, but then a-gain, no, or a

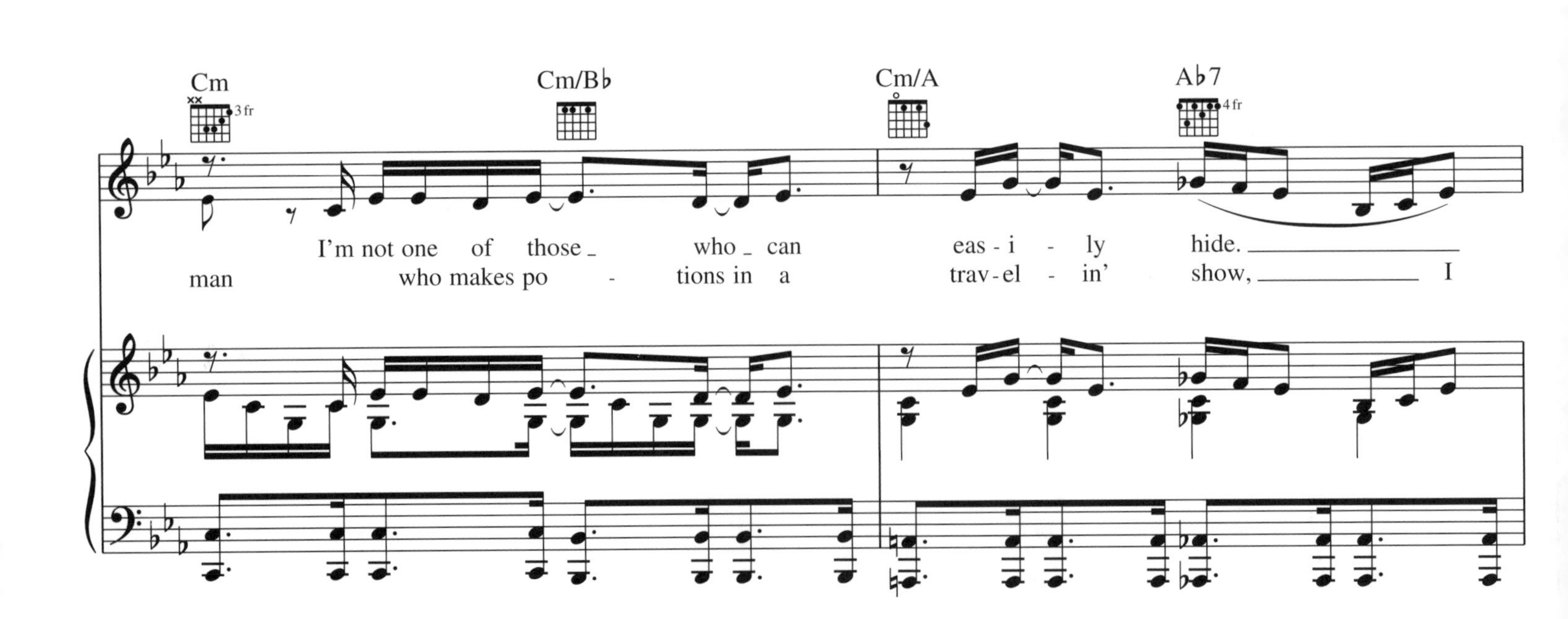
Cm
Cm/Bb
Cm/A
Ab7
3 fr
4 fr
I'm not one of those who can eas - i - ly hide.
man who makes po - tions in a trav-el - in' show, I

Eb/Bb
Bb
G/B
Cm
Don't have much mon - ey, but, boy, if I did,
know it's not much but it's the best I can do.
Eb
Fm7
1
Ab
Bb
I'd buy a big house where we both could live.
My gift is my song, and
Bbsus
Bb
2
Ab
Eb
this one's for you.
Ab/Eb
Eb
Bb/D
Cm
And you can tell ev - 'ry - bod - y

Fm7
Ab
Bb/D
Cm
this is your song.
It may be quite simple, but
Fm7
Ab
Cm
Cm/Bb
now that it's done,
I hope you don't mind,
I hope you don't mind
Cm/A
Ab6
Eb/G
Ab6
that I put down in words
how wonder-ful life is while
rit.
Ab
Bb
Bbsus
Bb
you're in the world.
a tempo

E♭
A♭maj7
B♭/D
Gm
I sat on the roof and kicked off the moss; well, a
So ex-cuse me for - get-ting, but these things I do;
Cm
Cm/B♭
Cm/A
A♭7
few of the vers - es, well, they've got me quite cross.
You see I've for-got-ten if they're green or they're blue.
E♭/B♭
B♭
G/B
Cm
But the sun's been quite kind while I wrote this song;
An - y - way, the thing is, what I real - ly mean,
E♭
Fm7
A♭
B♭
it's for peo-ple like you that keep it turned on.
yours are the sweet - est eyes
3fr
4fr
6fr

B♭sus
B♭
2
A♭
E♭
I've ev - er seen.
A♭/E♭
E♭
B♭/D
Cm
And you can tell ev - 'ry - bod - y
Fm7
A♭
B♭/D
Cm
this is your song.
It may be quite sim-ple, but
Fm7
A♭
Cm
Cm/B♭
now that it's done,
I hope you don't mind, I hope you don't mind

Cm/A
Ab6
3 fr
Eb/G
3 fr
Ab6
3 fr
that I put down in words how won - der - ful life is while
rit.
1
Ab
4 fr
Bb
Bbsus
Bb
you're in the world.
a tempo
2
Ab
4 fr
Eb
3 fr
Ab/Eb
you're in the world.
a tempo
Bb/Eb
Ab/Eb
Eb
3 fr

YOU SHOOK ME ALL NIGHT LONG

Words and Music by ANGUS YOUNG,
MALCOLM YOUNG and BRIAN JOHNSON

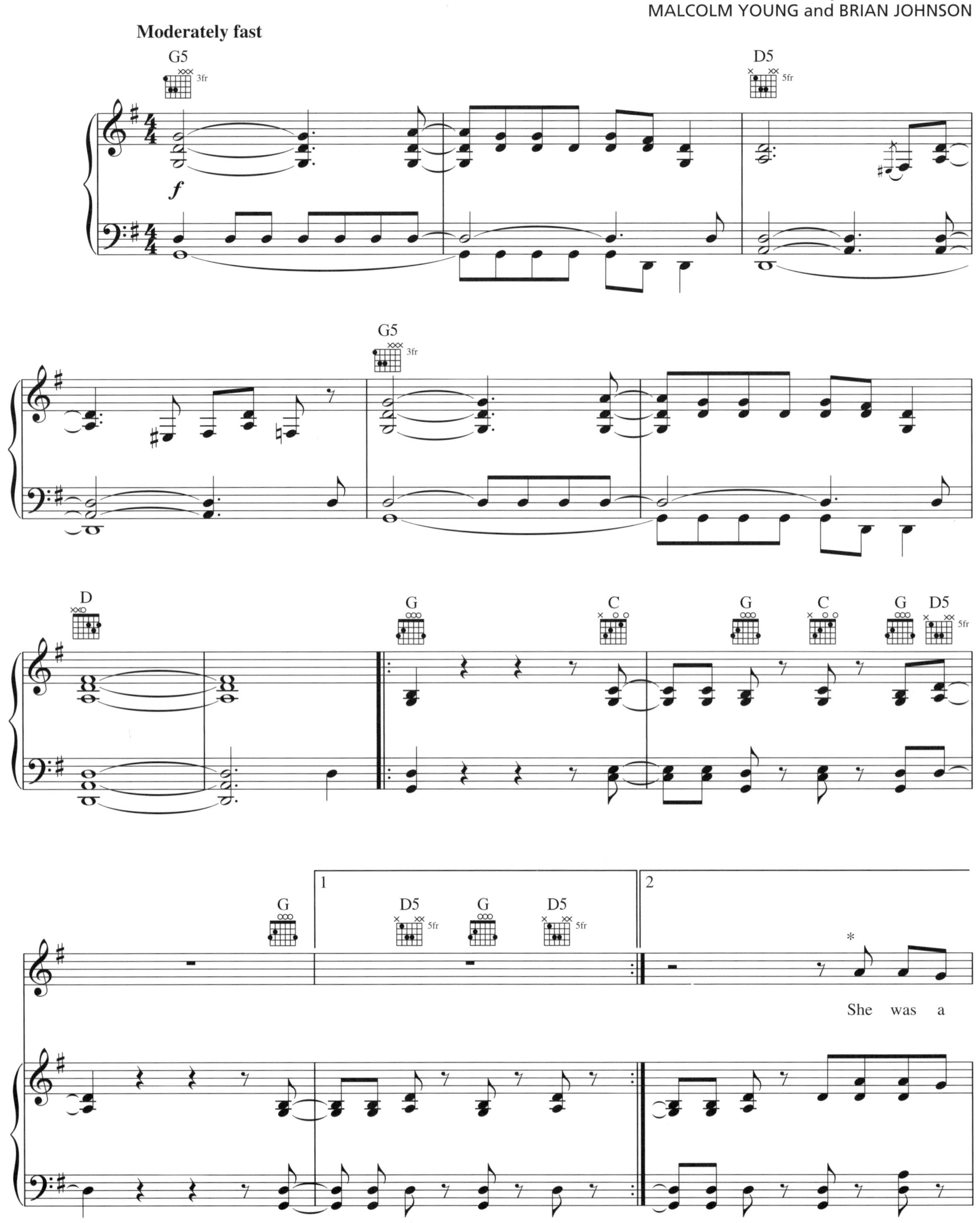

* Vocal written at pitch.

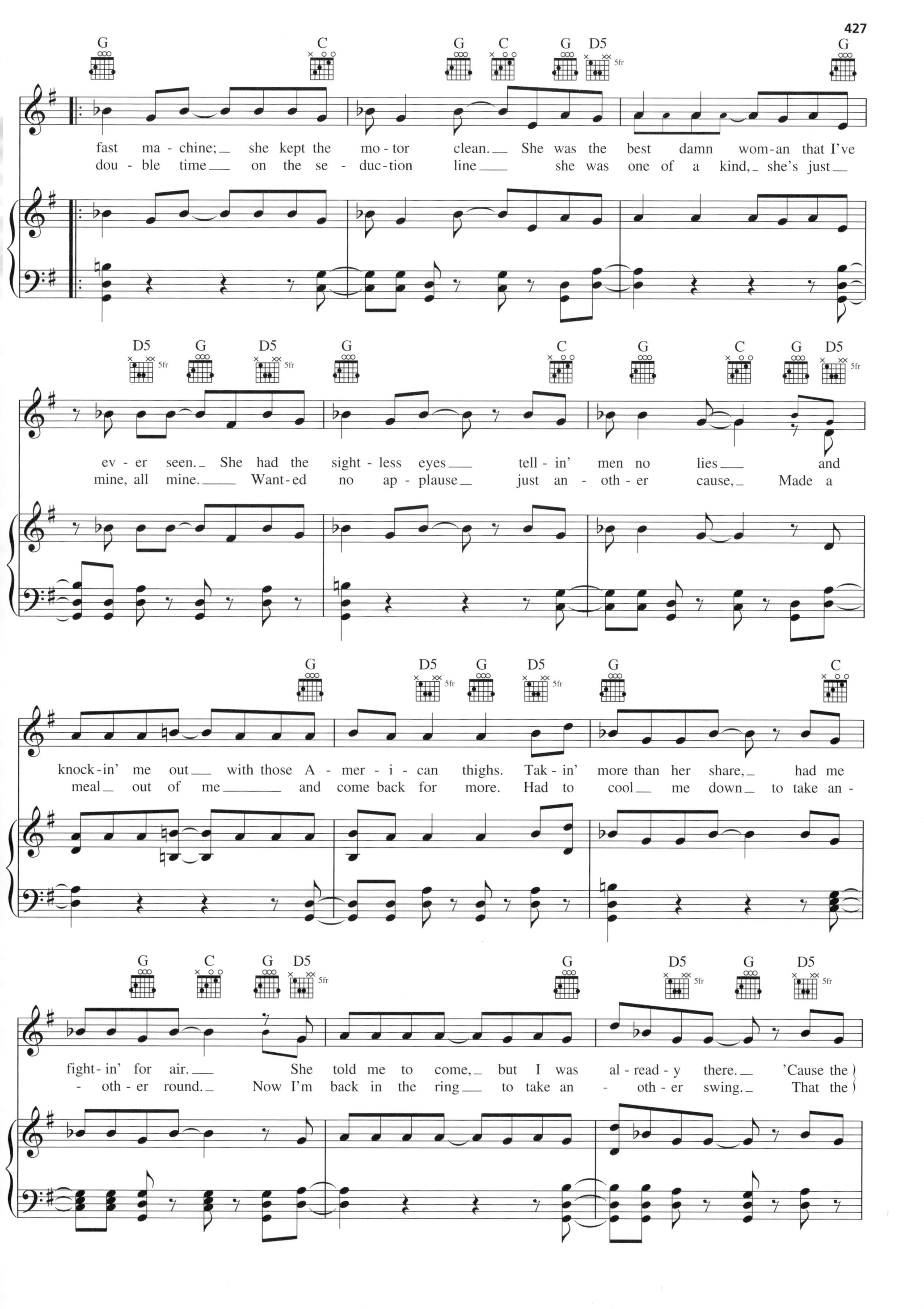
G C G C G D5 G
fast ma - chine; she kept the mo - tor clean. She was the best damn wom-an that I've
dou - ble time on the se - duc - tion line she was one of a kind, she's just
D5 G D5 G C G C G D5
ev - er seen. She had the sight - less eyes tell - in' men no lies and
mine, all mine. Want - ed no ap - plause just an - oth - er cause, Made a
G D5 G D5 G C
knock - in' me out with those A - mer - i - can thighs. Tak - in' more than her share, had me
meal out of me and come back for more. Had to cool me down to take an -
G C G D5 G D5 G D5
fight - in' for air. She told me to come, but I was al - read - y there. 'Cause the
- oth - er round. Now I'm back in the ring to take an - oth - er swing. That the
5fr

G
C
G
C
G
D5
5fr
Dsus
walls start shak - in', the earth was quak - in', my mind was ach - in' and
D5
5fr
Dsus
D5
5fr
G5
3fr
Csus
3fr
G/B
D
we were mak - in' it. And you shook me all night long.
Csus2
3fr
G/B
G5
3fr
Csus2
3fr
Yeah, you shook me all
G/B
D
1
Csus2
3fr
G/B
night long.
Work - in'

2
C
G/B
G5
Csus2
3fr
You knocked me out. I said you shook me all
G/B
D
Csus2
G/B
night long.
You had me shak - in', and
G5
Csus2
G/B
D5
G/D
5fr
you shook me all night long.
D5
Yeah, you shook me.
The way you took me.

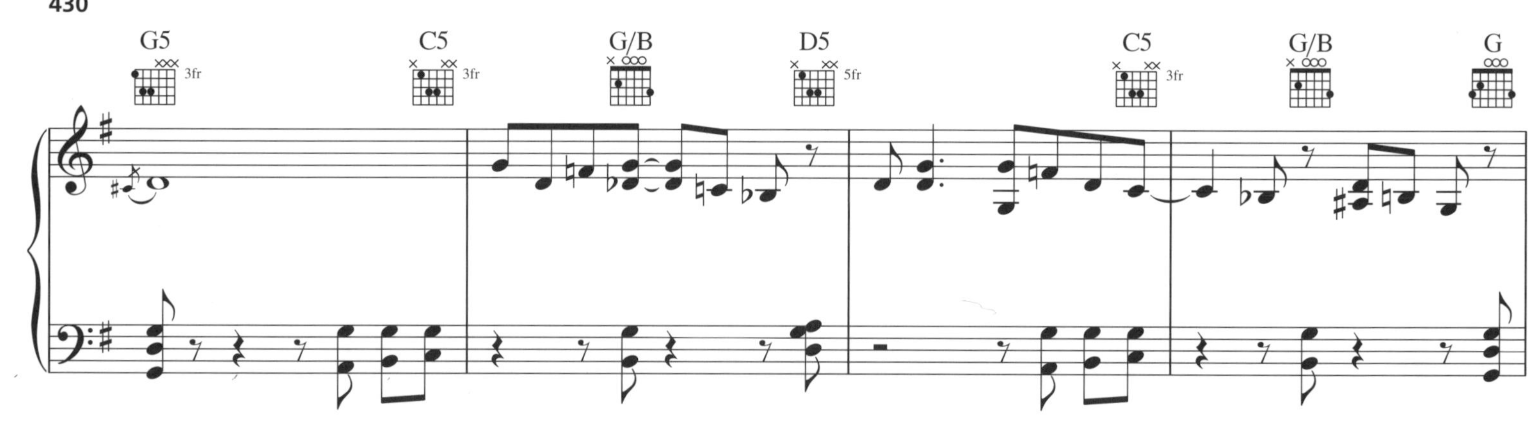
G5
3fr
C5
3fr
G/B
D5
5fr
C5
3fr
G/B
G

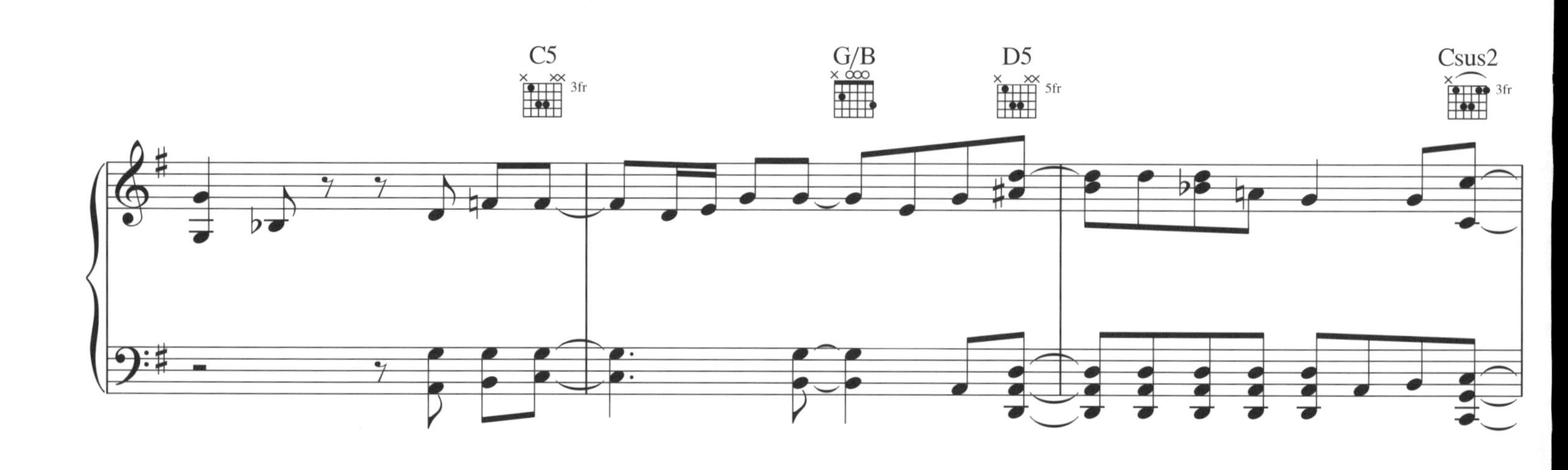
C5
3fr
G/B
D5
5fr
Csus2
3fr

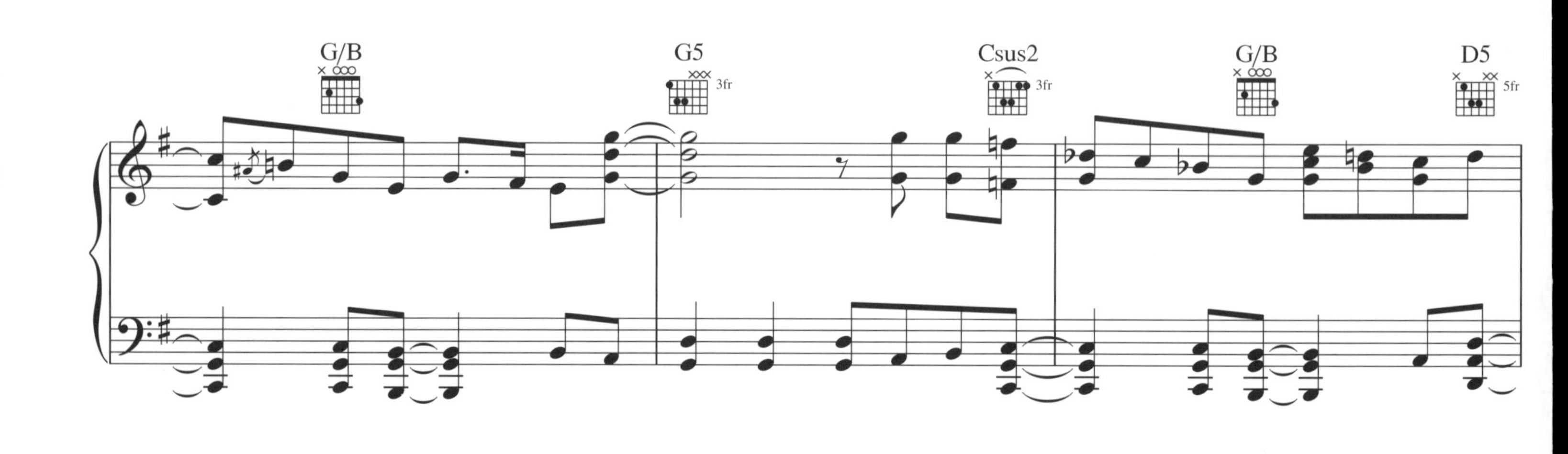
G/B
G5
3fr
Csus2
3fr
G/B
D5
5fr

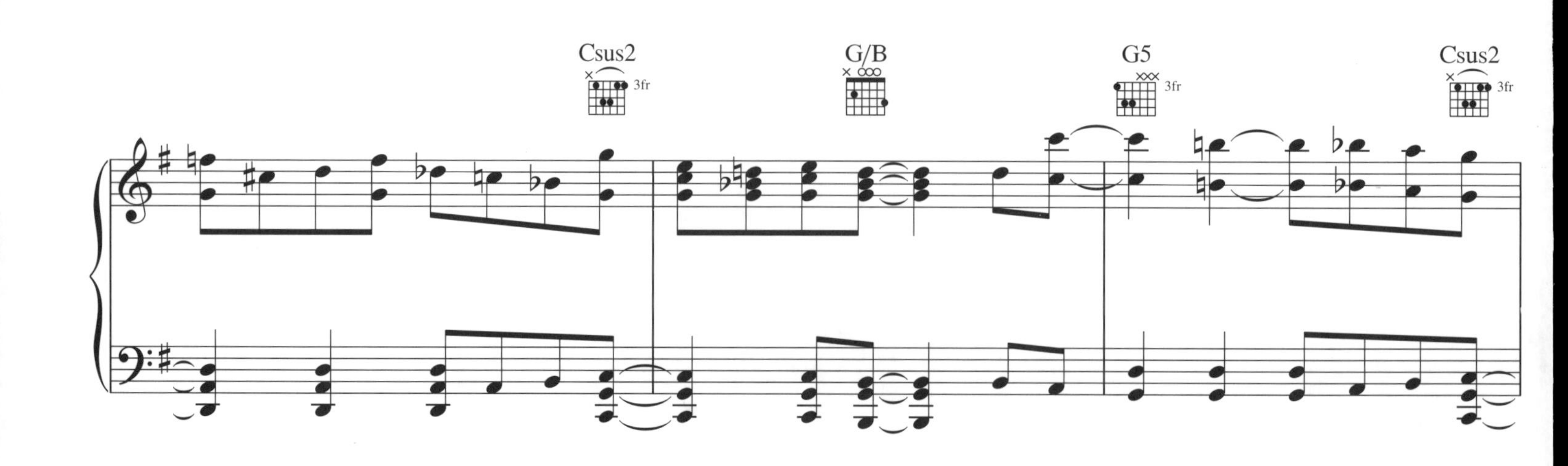
Csus2
3fr
G/B
G5
3fr
Csus2
3fr

G/B
D5
5fr
Csus2
3fr
G/B
You real - ly took me and
G5
3fr
Csus2
3fr
G/B
D
Csus2
3fr
you shook me all night long.
G/B
G
Csus2
3fr
G/B
D
3
3
Oh you shook me all night
Csus2
3fr
G/B
G5
3fr
C
long. Yeah, yeah, you shook me all

G/B
D
Csus2
G/B
night
long.
You real - ly got me and
G5
Csus2
G/B
D5
Csus2
you
shook me all
night
long.
G/B
D5
Csus2
G/B
D5
Yeah, you shook me.
Yeah, you shook me
all
night
long.